Education and Employment

Education and Employment

A Future Perspective of
Needs, Policies, and
Programs

Russell G. Davis
Gary M. Lewis
Harvard University

Lexington Books
D.C. Heath and Company
Lexington, Massachusetts
Toronto   London

Library of Congress Cataloging in Publication Data

Davis, Russell G.
    Education and employment.

    Bibliography: p.
    Includes index.
    1. Education—Economic aspects—United States. 2. Manpower policy—
United States. I. Lewis, Gary M., joint author. II. Title.
LC66.D39   331.1   74-28973
ISBN 0-669-98087-0

Published simultaneously in Canada.

Printed in the United States of America.

International Standard Book Number: 0-669-98087-0

Library of Congress Catalog Card Number: 74-28973

To my father, Edward W. Davis,

To my wife, Dorothy Milligan Lewis

Contents

List of Figures

List of Tables

Preface

The object of this study is to examine projected changes in the population and economy of the United States over the next fifteen-year period, and to trace the implications of such changes for employment and education policies and programs. Changes in the size and structure of the population will have clear and direct effects on the amount and kind of education and training people will want and need. Changes in the economy and work force will require changes in policies and programs designed to relate education to work. The objectives of education are broader than the preparation of workers, but it is this narrower concern that will receive major attention in this study.

This book is based mainly on projections of future employment that were run before the present depressed times and heavy unemployment that began in 1974. At the time the projections were made in 1973, mainly by the Bureau of Labor Statistics, inflation seemed the main problem in the short run and slowing growth in national output and employment the major problem over the long run. The slowing growth in the economy had clear consequences for slowing growth in employment and special problems for highly educated people who would be entering the work force in the years ahead. The sudden and dramatic worsening of general employment rates, which came in 1974, was not even imagined by the forecasters. Most of their projections were based on an assumption of an unemployment rate that would climb slightly above 4 percent. By the end of 1974 the unemployment rate was twice that rate, the highest since the years before World War II, when the country was just emerging from the Great Depression. Given the current employment crisis, the job and education future that is projected through most of this study may even be conservative or optimistic. It is unlikely that the present high rates will persist, but though unemployment declines the problem of diminished employment opportunity for college graduates that is envisaged for the future will remain. In the years ahead the problem will be getting a job. Of that there is little doubt.

Education must change to meet a changing demographic and economic demand. The latter demand has particular relevance for vocational or work-related education and training, especially for more recent program developments covered under the term *career education*. One of the simpler definitions of career education is offered by Hoyt, Evans, Mackin, and Mangum, who see it as "the total effort of public education and the community to help all individuals become familiar with the values of a work-oriented society, to integrate these values into their personal value systems, and to implement these values into their lives in such a way that work becomes possible, meaningful, and satisfying to each individual."[1] The terms *work-related education* and *work-based education* will also be used in the study, and will not be exactly synonymous with more traditional terms such as *occupational, vocational, trade* and *industrial* and *technical* education or training. Work-based education will mean exactly what the term suggests, education or training that is directly based in and on the production process itself. Examples range from on-the-job and apprenticeship programs to the *nai talim* (new education) of Gandhi, where the schools were envisaged as production enterprises, and the programs of the Chinese in the Yenan period where the slogans "study what you do and do what you study" describe the underlying notion. *Career education* is the newest term in the lexicon, and covers, as the definition suggests, a much broader objective than direct preparation for work.

Whether or not career education lasts, as a term or a policy, in the future there will be a form of education that is shaped primarily around the objective of preparing people for work, jobs, and careers. Such programs will be central to formal and nonformal schooling, although not the be-all and end-all of schooling and education. Schooling has been conceived, in times past, as having many objectives and offering many returns to participants. The lore of stable cultures has been preserved and transmitted to successive generations, and cultures have inevitably included more than work and production. Knowledge and culture have been expanded through scholarship and schooling. Elites have been trained for leadership through formal study; and specialized practitioners of the sciences and of the arts have been trained in general educational programs. More recently, populations in the mass have been socialized, and national identities and purposes forged through schooling. Ethics, aesthetics, and ideology have been disseminated through formal schooling. However, in all cultures and polities some part of education and training has been directed to preparing people for work and for enhancing job performance and production. It is this kind of education that will receive major attention in the analysis to follow.

In broad fashion, Chapter 1 will trace demographic, economic, and educational trends that come out of the recent past and presage future developments in work and education in the United States. The object is to provide a context for developing programs that will blend work experience, education, and training. Chapter 1 provides a general problem setting for adapting education to job and career development. The perspective is toward the future. Chapter 2 develops detailed supporting analysis for this perspective, using demographic, economic, and educational projections that cover the next fifteen years, roughly from 1975 to 1990. Clearly these projections are founded on assumptions and must be hedged around with qualifications and disclaimers. We are into the long run where indeed we might all be dead, but we assume not.

Before developing program response possibilities in work and schooling for the future in the United States, examination of other experience may be useful. Two pools of experience may be fished, one historical and the other comparative. The future comes out of the present which comes out of the immediate past, which in turn has developed from initiatives of earlier times. History, then, provides a record of experience, useful for shaping present and future programs of work-related education. Equally valuable is comparative experience provided through a review of the attempts in other countries in recent times to make education and training more responsive to employment and production. Some of these attempts have been viewed as reforms. Chapter 3 sketches out a history of such attempts in the United States and in other countries, mainly India, China, and Russia. The historical and comparative discussions are neither comprehensive nor detailed, and are offered mainly to illuminate the future perspective which is the main concern of the study.

Chapter 4 traces the program responses for the future in work-related or career education. Change is suggested not only for schooling and training but also for the organization of work itself and the jobs and career lines which the economy provides. A final short chapter or end note is offered on recent legislation to provide employment, jobs, and job training.

The book is written primarily to provide a basis for research and development for policies and programs to relate work and education more effectively. As a concomitant benefit it is hoped that forecasts, rough-cut though they are, may be useful for institutions developing long-range program plans, and for individuals plotting study, work, and career plans for the future.

Acknowledgments

A work of this size and complexity is the product of many contributors. The bibliography acknowledges many of these. Special mention should be made of the Bureau of Labor Statistics, U.S. Department of Labor. We also wish to acknowledge support from the National Institute of Education, U.S. Department of Health, Education and Welfare. Research Contract NIE C 74-0131 furnished partial support for some of the basic research, but this work, of course, does not necessarily reflect the opinions or policies of NIE.

A number of individuals have contributed materially to the study. Thomas Welch worked with us in the preparation of early drafts of the material. We are indebted to Lloyd David for furnishing information on the development of vocational education in the United States. Edward Mackin of Olympus Research Corporation also provided basic information on career education programs. We also wish to acknowledge our typist, Corinne Murphy, whose skill and diligence throughout the manuscript preparation is greatly appreciated. Finally, grateful mention should be made of the assistance of Dottie Lewis in the preparation of tables and figures.

Education and Employment

1 Employment and Education: Immediate Past and Future in Overview

Introductory Note

This chapter will begin with a very general summary of demographic and economic trends, and trace some broad consequences for employment and education. A somewhat richer summary, with salient statistics, will follow in this chapter, but the supporting data and detailed projections will be deferred to the following chapter. The arrangement permits the reader to examine the future perspective at any order of generality or detail that seems suitable.

The Recent Past in General Perspective

Because the present and future must flow from the recent past, examination of the past three quinquenia, the period from 1960 to the present, is instructive. Population increased in size. The growth came from increased fertility. The yield was larger families, larger school-age population, and larger enrollments, increasing at primary-school level from the late forties into the early sixties, and increasing at secondary-school level in the early fifties and running almost to the present.

Enrollments were increasing at postsecondary level all during the period, in part because of an increased population base, as in primary and secondary schools, but in part also because of increased participation rates by the population of eighteen-to-twenty-four-year-olds. Rates of attendance at postsecondary schools are influenced by economic and social considerations, rather than being a direct function of age-group size as in the case of primary and secondary school. In general, however, enrollments at all levels of schooling were large and growing during the recent past. These are obvious facts, known and shown in Table 2-3 (p. 24) of the detailed analysis to follow.

Figure 1-1 shows the increase in enrollments in all institutions of higher education in the United States. From 1951 to 1971 the increase was from 2.1 million to 8.1 million, more than a threefold increase. The likelihood of continuing increases in higher education enrollments in the next fifteen years will be examined in the light of projected economic growth and concomitant demand in the labor force for workers with higher-education credentials. Economic demand is not the only determinant of college and university enrollments, but it does have a powerful effect, and this will in turn influence

1

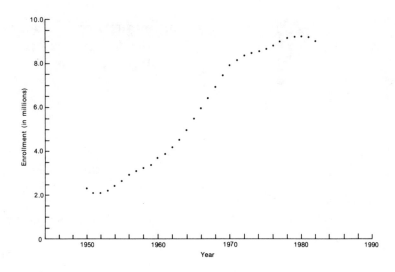

Figure 1-1: Degree-Credit Enrollment in All Institutions of Higher Education in the United States, Fall 1950-72, and Projected to 1982. Source: National Center for Educational Statistics, *Digest of Educational Statistics 1972*, table 87. U.S. Office of Education, *Projections of Educational Statistics to 1982-83*, table 6.

educational policies and individual decisions in the fifteen-year period ahead. It will also be interesting to examine whether recent stress on education and training directly relevant to employment and work will influence choice and enrollment in postsecondary programs.

The population grew and the economy grew over the past fifteen years, and increases in the GNP, and in the work force that produced it, were notable features of the period. Resources were available to support increased education at all levels, and growth in the population and GNP, except for short-term fluctuations in the latter, was fairly steady through the period. Until recent years the mood was expansive. Schools and colleges were built in time to the tempo of growth; training programs proliferated; bond issues were approved; teachers hired and institutions endowed. Then the pace began to slacken, beginning in primary school around 1968, and at secondary level only recently. These facts are also obvious and shown in Table 2-3 (p. 24). Enrollments in postsecondary institutions, especially in four-year degree programs, though not yet influenced by declining population in the age group, showed some tendency to dip at the very end of the recent period. The decline is of too short a duration to establish any clear future trends, but the possibility must be examined in the discussion to follow.

Table 2-3, however, also shows growth patterns that are not so obvious, but to examine them we must move from the recent past into the present and immediate future. There are also important trends that reflect changes in structure as well as size.

The Immediate Future

There will be another round of growth in population and school enrollments. As Table 2-3 indicates, it will begin in primary school around 1981 and continue for at least a decade; begin in secondary school in 1989, near the close of this forecast period, and continue until the end of the century. Whether it will continue in postsecondary schools and for how long is an interesting question, which will be examined later, but the implication of the primary- and secondary-school increases forecast for the future merit examination.

The future will not repeat itself in the matter of educational growth, even though straight demographic trends, and the numbers yielded may suggest so on the surface. Future growth rounds will be different in several important respects. From a demographic standpoint there will be a difference because the causes of the growth will be different. In the past, the growth resulted from high fertility which led to larger family size. Women of childbearing age had more children. In the future the growth will come from large numbers of women with low fertility, and the yield will be many but much smaller families. The large numbers of women coming into childbearing ages are members of the earlier large birth cohorts of the post-World War II years.

Though the numbers projected for school-aged populations and school enrollments may look the same, the family and school situation may be very different. There will be large numbers of children coming into primary-school age in the early eighties and into secondary-school age eight years later, but there may be no child-centered society of the fifties or youth culture of the sixties, for there will also be very large cohorts to be served in the twenty-five-to-forty-year-old age group. Although the problem of serving the child population will seem similar because of absolute magnitude, the situation could be very different in relative or structural terms, because of large populations in adult age groups. The age structure, relative numbers in the various age groups, will have important consequences for educational policies and programs. Policies will have to be designed to serve a bimodal client group, the school-age group, and a post-postsecondary clientele.

Programs and approaches will be different. Some implications for education and training are clear. Continuing or lifelong education, with open-entry, open-exit for older persons, will come, not because of the writing and urging of educators following the Faure Report,[1] but because the demographic situation indicates a substantial clientele in the older age groups who can and will demand educational services appropriate to their needs and condition. The problem of training large youth cohorts for entry-level employment, resulting in MDTA, Youth Corps, Job Corps, cooperative, work study, and prevocational training, will have to yield pride of place to policy and program concerns for in-job training and retraining of older and experienced workers. However, this must be a shift in relative and not absolute emphasis, given the inadequacy of most vocational programs of the recent past, even in purely quantitative terms. No more than a fraction of the potential need of youth for vocationally relevant training has ever been met, and this in turn will reinforce the demand for training for older age groups at a later time. There is a lot of unmet demand to pay for up ahead. Allocations will have to be split and program emphasis bifurcated. This would present no problem if resources were unlimited, but projections of economic performance indicate that this is not likely to be the case.

Other differences in program requirements may be implied by the size and age structure of the population forecast. How will children from small families and an adult-dominated society differ, and how will these differences be reflected in differing schooling needs? With less competition for parental attention in small families, language development could be more advanced; with less home contact with older siblings, social adjustment needs could be greater; with more working mothers, school service needs could expand or change. These possibilities are noted in passing, for here the focus of concern is more narrowly on work-based, rather than general, education.

The detailed analysis to follow will indicate a slowing economic growth. In part Bureau of Labor Statistics (BLS) projections of the economy are based on a slower growth of the population, and hence a slower increase in the work force and a slower rate of increase of product and income. This will be reinforced by resource scarcities in energy and raw materials and trade and monetary dislocations that are already appearing. The likelihood is that proportionate to the needs, less product, income, revenues and resources will be available for allocations to education and training. Withall, the work force is projected to increase from 86 million in 1970 to almost 113 million in 1990, and education and training establishments will have to serve a larger clientele in some fashion.

A General Summary of Demographic and Economic Trends

In general, forecasts of the population and the economy over the next fifteen years suggest that the education and training burden will be larger, much more complex in the sense of differing client groups to serve and needs to be met, and supported by resources that will be limited relative to the burden to be borne. Before offering detailed analysis to support these general observations, a summary of changes in the population and economy as projected by the Bureau of Labor Statistics may be helpful. From these "indications," certain general consequences for education and training may follow. In the next chapter more detailed analysis will provide the basis for more specific policy and program recommendations.

Population

Size and Growth. From an estimated 208.8 million people in 1972, the U.S. population is expected to grow to 246.6 million by 1990. This represents an overall cumulative annual rate of change of 0.9 percent between 1972 and 1990. The major reason for this growth occurs because of the very large numbers of women in prime child-bearing years. Women 20-34 years old are expected to increase from about 23 million in 1972 to over 30 million in 1985. These women will bear large numbers of children despite low fertility. (The total fertility rate assumed in these demographic projections by the US Bureau of the Census is the replacement rate of 2.1 births per woman over her child-bearing years, but already the figure is below this in the short term. In 1973 the total fertility rate was 1.9.)

Structure: Age, Sex, and Race. In general the ethnic and sex structure of the population will not be appreciably different over the forecast period. Male/ female proportions will be roughly the same, with the usual slight preponderance of females. The higher fertility rates for nonwhites are likely to move closer to lower figures for whites, but for the forecast period there will still be larger proportions of nonwhites in lower age groups in comparison to the higher age groups. Currently some 15.8 percent of the total population under 16 years of age is nonwhite, compared to only 11.6 percent for those 16 and older.

The age structure of the population shows some definite trends that will have implications for education and training. The age group of those 16 and below is expected to decline from 61 to 57 million during 1972-80 and to rise slowly to 63.6 million by 1990. Those 20-34 years old will increase in numbers from 45.6 million in 1972 to 61.2 million in 1985 and then decline to about 60 million in 1990 as the baby boom bulge passes on to the next age group. The 35-54 age group will increase steadily, from 46.4 million in 1972 to 61.5 million in 1990. In general the average age of the population will rise over the forecast period. Those under 16 years old will fall from 29.2 percent to 25.8 percent of the total population over the period.

Economic Activity

Size and Growth. From a base year figure of $1155.2 billion in 1972, the gross national product of the U.S. is expected to reach $1657.9 billion in 1980 and

$1942.5 billion by 1985. This represents an average annual rate of growth of 4.6 percent over the period 1972-80, but only 3.2 percent over the period from 1980 to 1985. In general there will be a slowing growth rate over the forecast period. Note, however, the slowing growth rate in the economy when compared to the even slower growth rate in the population will yield a more favorable per capita income for the period. Note also that this means nothing about the distribution of income.

Structure: Percent Contribution to GNP by Sectors. BLS projections show the following changes in contributions to GNP by various sectors: agriculture declining from 3.4 percent of GNP in 1972 to 2.1 percent in 1985; manufacturing falling very little, from 28.5 percent to 28.2 percent over the same period; "other services" rising from 13.3 percent in 1972 to 15.3 percent in 1985; trade declining slightly; transportation rising slightly; construction declining.[2]

Labor Force and Employment

Size and Growth. In general there is an expected slowing labor force growth rate beyond 1980. The estimated 1970 labor force was 85.9 million, which is projected to increase to 101.8 million by 1980, and to 112.6 million by 1990. This represents an average annual rate of change of 1.7 percent between 1970 and 1980 and only 1.0 percent from 1980 to 1990.

Employment by Sectors. The overall average annual rate of change in employment is expected to be 2.2 percent from 1972-80 and 1.2 percent from 1980-85. In general employment growth will slow in all sectors, but the magnitude will vary by sector. The average annual change in employment in government is projected to be 2.8 percent from 1972-80 and 2.5 percent from 1980-85; in manufacturing to be 2.2 percent from 1972-80 and 0.5 percent from 1980-85; in "other services" to be 3.1 percent from 1972-80 and 1.9 percent over the period 1980-85; but to be −4.9 percent during 1972-80 and −3.7 percent from 1980-85 in the agricultural sector. (These projections were run before the present abrupt declines of early 1975.)

Unemployment. There is no useful projection for unemployment, inasmuch as this is assumed at 4 percent in basic projections. The future burden of unemployment should be more evenly distributed across age and ethnic groupings, and fall less heavily on youth and the nonwhite, but this will not happen without continuing enforcement of antidiscrimination regulations and explicit program attention. Currently a 4 percent unemployment rate seems impossibly low.

Labor Force Structure: Race and Sex. There will be no remarkable changes in the racial and sex structure of the labor force. However, female participation rates may increase faster than detailed projections show. Increased entry of women and nonwhites into certain occupational groups is not shown clearly in the forecasts.

Occupational Structure. In general there will be high job growth and replacement needs for white-collar workers (professional, managerial, sales, and clerical). Blue-collar employment growth and replacement will represent only 36 percent of the growth and replacement expected for white-collar workers, with the largest total blue-collar job openings over the forecast period occurring in the crafts and operatives categories.

Varied average annual rates of change of employment by occupation are projected. Even during the years of slow economic growth projected for 1980-85 the average annual rate of change in employment for professional and technical workers is expected to be 2.5 percent. This is a decline from an expected 3.5 percent annual rate of increase over the period from 1972 to 1980. At the other extreme are farmworkers, whose employment levels are expected to continue falling. Other occupational categories generally will increase, but at varying rates. Managers and administrators are expected to increase at an average annual rate of 2.8 percent from 1972 to 1980 and by 0.8 percent per year from 1980 to 1985. Sales workers are expected to show a similar pattern: increasing by 2.1 percent per year over the period 1972-80 and only by 0.5 percent annually from 1980 to 1985. Operatives, as well as craft and kindred workers, are projected to increase at a 1.6 percent annual growth rate from 1972 to 1980, but operatives are expected to experience the more rapid decline in growth in the eighties. The BLS has projected that employment for operatives will increase by 0.5 percent per year from 1980 to 1985, while craft and kindred worker employment will grow at 1.2 percent per year over the same period. Employment in service occupations is expected to be somewhat more resistant to the slow economic growth expected from 1980 to 1985. Whereas the projected average annual rate of change in service jobs is 1.9 percent over 1972-80, it will fall to only 1.0 percent during 1980-85.

Education and Training

Primary and Secondary Education. There will be a declining population of six-year-olds entering primary schools from the present until 1980, and a rising population base from 1981 to 1991. Total primary-school enrollments will follow these trends, lagged by a few years. There will be a declining population of fourteen-year-olds entering secondary schools from 1976 to 1988, and a rising trend again from 1989 to the end of the century. Total secondary-school enrollments will follow these trends, lagged by a few years. Absolute enrollments will not reach the numbers reached in the 1950-60 period.

Postsecondary Education. The 18-year-old age group population will be declining from 1980 to 1992 and then rising to the end of the century. Enrollments at the postsecondary level are not wholly dependent on age-group population, and depend on participation rates which now show a short-term decline. The percent of high-school seniors enrolled in higher education in the fall of their year of graduation has fallen from 55 percent to 49 percent in four years. The rate of increase in the percentage of the age group graduating from high school is also slowing as it moves toward an upper limit between 90 and 100 percent. Of three available projections of university enrollments, the U.S. Office of Education, Carnegie, and U.S. Census, indications are that the lowest rate may prevail, yielding total degree and nondegree enrollment in higher education of about 10.4 million by the end of the forecast period in 1990.

Educational Attainment in the Labor Force. Based on the 1972 U.S. Office of Education projections of school enrollments, the Bureau of Labor Statistics has projected these changes in educational attainment in the labor force:

Attainment Level	Percent Change in the Labor Force
4+ years of college	Increasing from 14.6 percent in 1970 to 23.8 percent in 1990
1-3 years college	Increasing from 12.0 percent in 1970 to 16.4 percent in 1990
4 years high school	Increasing from 37.5 percent in 1970 to 41.2 percent in 1990
Less than 4 years of high school	Decreasing from 35.9 percent in 1970 to 18.6 percent in 1990

In general low educational attainment will be concentrated in the higher age groups in the labor force. This will be a small but highly disadvantaged client group, requiring special attention.

Supply and Demand for Higher Education. BLS projections are for an oversupply of 700,000 college graduates in the 1980-85 period. This is based on the comparison of the educational requirements of jobs and continued high enrollments in postsecondary educational institutions. However, lower projections of enrollments (see above) indicate that this oversupply will not appear if present short-term trends of declining enrollments in regular four-year colleges continue. Note that one likely possibility is a shift from four-year general college to shorter, more vocationally relevant postsecondary training, or short period education interspersed with work experience.

Training for Employment. The federal government, through OEO, MDTA, emergency and comprehensive training programs, and more recently out of the Comprehensive Employment and Training Act (CETA, 1973), has sponsored and supported a variety of emergency job-creation and training programs. Estimating the coverage and projecting the supply of trainees from such programs is not possible, since the legislation permits the expansion of training programs in response to economic condition, i.e. pegs the program build-up in areas according to rises in unemployment. In the recent past many such programs have been declining, and on the basis of scattered evidence, present coverage does not appear to be meeting demand for vocational training.[3]

In 1973, with a potential unemployed target group of 4.3 million (and with another 6.7 million out of the labor force or underemployed), about 1.5 million were accommodated in such programs as institutional training, JOP-OJT, NYC, Mainstream, PSC, CEP, JOBS, etc. Most state surveys indicate a substantial clientele that cannot now be served in existing vocational-training, manpower-training, and career-education programs. The numbers accommodated in proportion to age-group sizes are very small. In 1974 Massachusetts offered only 300 enrollment places in Operation Mainstream; 5 percent of the students enrolled in General Curriculum in Massachusetts are to be covered in occupational programs by 1976; and Work Study and Cooperative Education programs in that state move from a coverage of about 0.5 percent of the age group in 1973 to 1 percent in 1978.

Inadequate coverage appears to be generally prevalent throughout the country, although data to support this assertion are not clear on a national basis.

Work-Related Education in Fifteen-Year Perspective: A Summary

The summary of demographic, economic, and educational trends offers a variety of policy and program response possibilities. Here the emphasis will be on employment creation, job development and enhancement, and education and training that contribute maximally to these ends. The objectives of education go beyond preparing citizens for work, just as the creation and enhancement of employment require policies and programs that lie outside of education and training narrowly defined. Career education, embracing as it must all modes and means for preparing the members of our society for productive and satisfying work, intersects employment and education. Outside the area of intersection there is much of education that is not directly aimed at preparing people for work. In the larger area of employment creation, there are substantial areas of policy concern that do not fall within the domain of education.

Employment Creation and Education for
Employment

Figure 4-1 (p. 86) attempts to schematize the situation. To the right of the program possibilities for educating and training people to get jobs, develop and progress in the jobs, and attain satisfaction through work, there appears a summary list of the kinds of government and private policies and programs necessary to create and enhance employment. Possibilities range from broad monetary and fiscal policies aimed at stimulating spending, economic activity, and increasing employment, to direct government intervention through public employment and youth mobilization programs. Possibilities will be discussed in greater detail in a later section on policies and programs.

Even a glimpse of the future state of the economy indicates that the creation of jobs must be a primary policy goal. Given the size of the future population, the large numbers in prime working years, the slow growth of the economy and work force, and the potential oversupply of highly educated female and male workers, the great prize of the future may be a job; and securing a job that rewards commensurately to talent and training may be the prize of prizes. If increased enrollment in professional schools and postsecondary training institutions, decreased enrollments in general education, and increased competition for grades are signs, young people may already be aware of the job problem ahead. The trends indicated may be by no means healthy or wise, but the signs are appearing, at least in the short run. Concerns of young people appear to be changing from the political and social preoccupations of the sixties to the occupational orientation of earlier times. For many, the children of the ethnic minorities and the less privileged among the majority, the concern has never been different. Hence, in the future as in the present, no provision of educational and training opportunity will compensate for a lack of provision for creation of employment in the first place, and for investment to improve basic employment through the redesign of work, job development, and enrichment. Save for a small minority of the affluent and a small group so oppressed by circumstances that hope for securing meaningful work died early, there has never been any evidence that securing financially and psychically rewarding work has *not* been a major goal of Americans. The quest for rewarding work is likely to be just as central in the years ahead, and in fact the (relative) scarcity of work, given the supply of jobs and the numbers to fill them, is likely to make it even more of a desired end.

Thus the basis for any meaningful set of policies, programs, and allocations priorities for work-related education must be:

1. Maximization of employment opportunities through job creation.
2. Enhancement of employment opportunities through job enrichment.
3. Equitable distribution of job opportunities and the earning benefits derived from them.
4. Accomplishment of these objectives in a way that will not reduce economic output below a point where employment, job opportunities, and earnings benefits are in the long run reduced.

The last condition imposes severe limits on the extent to which an economy can explicitly and independently concentrate on employment maximization and equitable distribution of benefits, for unless other policies and conditions are in appropriate constellation, resulting inflation, reduced productivity, and diminished output may in the long course slow economic growth and reduce employment and earnings benefits. The mobilization of the society and enforcement of controls so as to attain a semblance of equity in the distribution of limited product is an alternative, but over the brief period of the forecast does not seem likely. For the immediate future it is likely that the known policies, however imprecise their effects may be gauged, will prevail.

The four basic points that must underlie employment and education policies, though obvious, have consequences that are not so obvious. Shifting public attention and support, as well as individual concern, away from educational opportunity and toward job opportunity could have lasting consequences for educational institutions as they now are organized and run. Short-run economic gains and efficiencies may be gained at the expense of lasting cultural and social loss both for individuals and institutions. Though a program of public investment directly in job creation and enhancement, rather than more indirectly in general education, seems sensible, the concomitant reduction of allocations to educational institutions and individual scholarship support may be far less attractive. Though the demographic indications are that there will be substantial school-age population growth beginning early in the eighties and flowing along through successively higher grade levels until the end of the century, and though it is unlikely that allocations will not be forthcoming to provide basic education for the young, and to provide teaching employment for substantial numbers of educated adults, allocations for higher education as conventionally offered now do not seem as persuasive a case, either on the basis of economic demand for educated workers, or on the basis of diminished revenues from a slowly growing economy. Given this situation, investment in jobs rather than higher education may appear very reasonable.

However, because the effectiveness of investment programs for job creation is no easier to assess than the effectiveness of investment in general education, the argument for any given program will not be indisputably clear, and there is just as much danger of wasting resources on one as the other. The yield of job-creation programs in countries where they have been tried, India being a major example, is meager. Past programs attempted through a partnership between private industry and government in the United States do not appear to have been very effective, and pure government-created mass employment has a history of mixed success that will be briefly reviewed later. Still, since some move in this direction seems likely, policies and programs must be developed, tried, and improved so as to return the best yield possible; and educational institutions must face the possibility of reduced attention and support and change accordingly. To temper the effects of shifting support, some countervailing policies and support programs for institutions offering general education may have to be devised, so that adjustments can be made over time.

Given limited resources and the possibility of substantial allocations to direct job creation and enhancement, large requirements for providing basic schooling for increasing numbers of children in the eighties, and limited resources for public programs of all kinds, it is essential that the large numbers of men and women workers in the 25-45 age groups be offered the most cost-effective work-related education and training possible. Though the demographic projections indicate large numbers moving through the prime working-age groups during the forecast period, the full measure of the burden is not revealed by numbers of people alone. The labor-force projections indicate a very substantial demand for educated and trained workers. Presumably, the provision of educated workers to produce the increased product, and to fill the increased requirements opened by growth and replacement needs for white collar workers of the service sector, will be met through the very large numbers forecast to come out of institutions of higher education (even under the most moderate assumptions of growth). This is one reason allocations will not shift too abruptly away from higher education, especially in the professional schools and occupational-training programs. There is the additional economic benefit resulting from new knowledge produced in universities and applied through research and development in technology to the enhancement of production and the more effective management of the economy. Institutions of higher education are not likely to be starved for support in the future, but future policies for supporting them may have to be based on the provision of more short courses designed to offer specific training for specific job-performance needs. In turn these segments may have to be bound into programmatic sequences that run over several years; and with special-purpose training interwoven with general studies, again arranged in shorter modules. Between actual resident study sequences there may have to be arrangements for self-study and institutional monitoring. The instructional technology is available to sustain such learning sequences, but the overall design of curricula will present challenging tasks and demand creative flexible instructional responses in order to avoid mere aggregates of academic bits and pieces. The great age of faith in general education may not be ended, but new work-based offerings may have to be part of the programs of even the most prestigious universities.

There will still be substantial support for many programs of higher education. Investment in occupational and professional training for service workers, unlike the case in large industry, is a form of investment in job creation, given rising incomes or subsidies sufficient to enable clients to purchase the services offered. The same is also true of support for self-employment enterprises in small industry and commerce for which proprietors and managers must be trained. Assuming that postsecondary schooling will more than supply the 18 million professional, technical, and managerial job growth and replacement requirements between 1972 and 1985, training of the 17 million clerical and kindred workers will still provide a formidable task order to the appropriate training establishments. For those clerical occupations for which the Bureau of Labor Statistics has made detailed employment projections, there are expected to be an average of 919,200 annual openings due to growth and replacement over the forecast period 1972-85.[4] Training completions from junior colleges (1970-71), MDTA training (FY 1973), Job Corps (FY 1972), and vocational education at the secondary and postsecondary level (FY 1972) totaled 801,000.[5] The occupational supply figure, however, does not include completions from private vocational schools or home study courses, sources that could be expected to narrow somewhat the gap between supply and anticipated demand.

The forecasts also indicate a large number of craftsmen and skilled workers needed to produce the industrial product that will still represent over a quarter of the GNP in the 1980s. By 1985 almost 13.8 million blue-collar workers will be required to meet the job growth and replacement needs of the work force, and about 5.3 million must be skilled (see Table 2-13, p. 42). For those craft and kindred occupations that the Bureau of Labor Statistics has made detailed employment projections, there are expected to be an average of 368,100 annual openings due to growth and replacement from 1972 to 1985.[6] Training completions from junior colleges (1970-71), MDTA training (FY 1973), Job Corps (FY 1972), vocational education at the secondary and postsecondary level (FY 1972), and apprenticeship programs (1972) totaled 186,300.[7] Other formal or informal employer occupational training and completions from private vocational schools could be expected to narrow the gap between supply and expected demand, but given the present size of vocationally directed education and training programs, there would seem to be a substantial need for increased support of such programs over the coming years. However, if jobs are scarce and of central concern, labor market demand will control training program design.

The issue for future policy and program development is whether those programs and the policies that will govern their growth and development in the coming years are appropriate to the needs of the economy, the numbers and kinds of clients to be educated, and the program arrangements that best prepare the individual clients to the tasks they must perform in the work force. Having established this, it is appropriate to fit program requirements to the resources that will be available to meet them.

Future policies and programs for employment creation, job enhancement, and work-related education and training must be shaped on these bases:

1. The numbers, types, characteristics, and needs of the people to be served. This covers student/trainee worker traits and needs and employer preferences.

2. The characteristics of the economy, and more specifically:

a. numbers required in the work force according to economic activity and occupational structure.
b. product and revenue yield to support employment and educational programs.

3. The program content and arrangements that provide the best fit between 1 and 2. This will be powerfully influenced by a perceived need for clients to hold on to their job base and to adapt their education and training plans to their employment status.

A Profile of Future Work and Education Arrangements

Already we have some profile of the demographic, economic, and educational future that may provide guidance for a first-order shaping of policies and programs. Later analysis will deepen and detail this first approximation:

1. There must be heavy emphasis on policies which create jobs, both entry-level opportunities for the young and new jobs for men and women of mature years.

2. Job development and enrichment, the restructuring of work opportunities, will be as significant as job creation, and possibly demand more ingenuity, attention, and resources. Policies and programs for work redesign, job restructuring, and enrichment will be most difficult to develop, for it is here that limited experience must be supplemented by careful research, experimentation, and trial. The job and work requirements and preferences of managers/employers and employees/workers are not always in harmony, and resolution of this problem will be time-consuming and costly.

3. Development of self-employment opportunities in services, commerce, and small industry will contribute to both employment creation and job enrichment and satisfaction, and though the costs of training and support for such programs are high on a unit basis, the double yield will make the investment a productive one.

4. Provision of basic schooling for very large numbers of young people coming into school age after 1980 will compete for attention and resources with training and retraining of older groups.

5. Support for higher education in its more standard forms will be necessary because of the large requirements for advanced training of professional and

technical workers and for support of research and development to support technological advancement. Still, conventional university and colleges of general education may lose their traditional position of preeminence.

6. Support for continuing education and training at higher and middle levels will be necessary to fit the needs of large numbers of men and women already at work and unable or unwilling to interrupt their careers for full-time study. On-job experience and supervised performance, interspersed with short periods of general and specialized education, may be required in a new pattern somewhat different from traditional apprenticeship and more like continuing and cooperative education if current patterns were extended beyond the present primary focus on entry-level preparation, and more stress was placed on adaptation and actualization over a long period of career development.

7. Trade and technical education must have continuing emphasis for filling the large numbers of technical and skilled jobs.

8. Trade and technical education will have to be provided in a less rigid form to serve the older workers, and its features will be open/entry, open/exit, acceleration, piece-wise, job-based training carried on concurrently with production.

9. The same large numbers and similar client groups will have to be served by programs for training the large numbers required in clerical and kindred tasks.

10. Very large numbers of women will be in the work force at all levels, and with early-year exits and later re-entrance, the retraining burden will be heavy. The period of stay outside the work force will be shorter, but some attention will have to be given to insure that interruption of work does not penalize opportunities for full-career advancement.

11. The very large numbers of small families may mean that nonformal education in the home through increased parent-child interaction, supplemented by educational opportunities offered through the mass media, may take some of the basic developmental burden from conventional schooling.

12. With a high value on jobs and career opportunities, the kind of information and guidance programs that are now beginning in career education programs at elementary school level will attract increasing support and interest.

13. To maintain contact with reality and preserve an aura of meaningfulness and relevance to work, the career-education programs at the secondary level will have to be accompanied by work experience of the kind provided through cooperative and work-study programs. These programs will have to be redesigned, expanded, and improved over their present status, a point that will be developed in Chapter 4.

14. Though emphasis will shift to programs serving the career and vocational development of older clients, present programs for the young are still so small compared to potential clientele that there will be a continuing need to expand conventional training opportunities.

15. The expanded career-education and vocational-training opportunities are

likely to shift upward from secondary to postsecondary level, particularly in many technical and subprofessional fields. However, vocational training at secondary level will still be the only viable opportunity open to many groups, and though secondary-level programs may not expand rapidly, they are unlikely to decrease.

16. If trends continue, there may be less enrollment in general education at postsecondary level, but since this is a necessary base for education at the highest levels there must be continued support despite high unit costs and competition for support in other areas of need, i.e., employment creation, continuing education of adults, and specialized or vocationally directed training.

17. There are no indications that private enterprise will assume the major training burdens from public, and it is uncertain whether this should be encouraged. Instead a partnership which provides work sites for practice and apprenticeship in private enterprise, and supplementary schooling in the public institution, should continue to be encouraged. The problem is in devising effective incentives for encouraging this partnership.

18. With declining numbers of youth and new entries to the work force in the early and middle position of the forecast period, attention and resources can shift to some extent to the less familiar problems of on-job career development and the adaptive training appropriate to encourage it.

19. Though heavy subsidies may have to be paid out for job creation, in the form of incentives to employers or support for employees, the costs of job restructuring and development may be even larger, and could include short-term indirect costs of reduced production as well as costly information and education programs for employees and employers.

20. Public employment programs will be necessary intermittently and perhaps on a large scale during the period, and planning and preparation of works projects with high social yield and quick build-up potential should be an on-going activity, between periods when the programs are actually running. Each program should have a built-in retraining and readjustment-to-other-employment feature of the kind developed for assisting military and veterans in re-entry to the civilian labor force.

21. There will be substantial numbers needing special attention and program assistance during the early part of the forecast period:

a. Young ethnic and minority group members will still require substantial pre-employment assistance and support in early work experience.
b. Increased opportunities for work experience and cooperative education will have to be provided, especially to groups in small towns and rural areas where opportunities are scarce. These may be very high cost compared to similar programs in urban/industrial areas.
c. Though the numbers of older and less educated workers will be declining through worker death and retirement, there will still be substantial numbers

even at the end of the period, and special programs must be offered, perhaps at high unit costs because of the need for repeat retraining.

d. Training opportunities for women in the fields previously closed or restricted will have to be strongly supported.

e. There will be no lessening in the need for programs for the physically handicapped, although the numbers of young handicapped needing assistance may diminish.

22. Present pilot level and exemplary programs offering work experience and cooperative educational opportunities will have to be greatly expanded for:

a. Youth alternating between school and work site;

b. Women alternating between home and work site;

c. Handicapped people alternating between home and sheltered work site;

d. Institutionalized participants alternating between institution and work site;

e. Workers alternating between work site and training institution; and

f. Workers alternating among several work sites for career exploration and job enrichment. (These programs will be difficult to arrange, support, and develop; and costs may be high.)

23. The profession of training specialists and work/training coordinators will develop and attract highly talented people who might in the past have entered leadership posts in general education. Better training, selection, and credentialing procedures for these emerging specialties are needed.

24. Both schools and jobs will be much more open and less rigidly controlled, and though this will have obvious advantages, it will have considerable cost and require new forms of management.

25. One would hope for increased participation of groups and individuals in the development of work and schooling programs and schedules. This will not come easily or automatically and there must be information, training, practice, pilot trial, evaluation, and development over time. However, with larger numbers of older persons participating in the combination of schooling and job development, the resistance to greater participatory voice in program design and governance may be lessened. Career educational programs for the young at elementary school level should offer participatory experience earlier, when disruption and confusion are less costly to bear.

26. Just as there must be effective programs to prepare young people for employment, to help workers to adapt to the requirements of work, and to help adapt jobs to the developmental needs of workers, so there must be programs to help older workers leave employment and adapt to a life that is not wholly work based. With large numbers of men and women coming into earlier retirement, this adaptation away from the world of work will require substantial attention and support, and may be best developed as a late station in a program for winding down work habits through lifelong and continuing education.

27. As a result of increased enrollments beginning in primary schools in the early 1980s and extending into secondary schools by the early 1990s, an increased number of teachers may be needed at these levels. This could result from a combination of circumstances:

a. Absolute increases in enrollments.
b. Maintenance of low pupil/teacher ratios that have evolved during a period of declining enrollments. These lower ratios may be maintained through teacher unions and parental preferences.
c. Aging of the teacher force over years when new hiring of teachers has slowed.
d. Too slow a build-up of the supply of graduates from teacher-training institutions. This may result from inertia that exists in education, where adjustment to changed situations comes slowly. This may be the reverse side of the failure in the recent past to adjust teacher supply to falling demand.
e. New levels and kinds of attention required for socialization of children from large numbers of very small family units.

2

Detailed Analysis and Implications of Projections Concerning Population, the Economy, and Education

Introduction

Recent Bureau of Labor Statistics (BLS) forecasts indicate that colleges and universities, over the next fifteen-year period, will overproduce to the point where the United States economy will no longer be able to employ highly educated labor at commensurate levels of earning and job responsibility.[1] In the preceding chapter the same possibility was outlined. However, the general indications that come out of general projections, and the profiles of the future states of education and employment outlined in the preceding chapter, must be supported and in part qualified by more detailed examination of the demographic, economic, and educational trends that underlie broader predictive statements. No single set of predictive statements can be traced uniquely from the underlying trends, and it is possible to reach different conclusions from the same sets of data on which the trend analysis is based. The future will be shaped by millions of individual decisions about work and education, and conclusions from projections themselves can feed back into the system and influence the aggregate of decisions that are made. So, too, can policies and programs be introduced to change the direction of trends. Last and not least, unforeseen events in the world ahead can radically alter the individual decisions, the aggregate of decisions, and the policies and programs. Predicting an oversupply of college-trained workers is one way to forfend against this very thing happening; and no one is unhappy when a gloomy prediction is confounded by future events, least of all those who make the predictions.

Collegiate Expansion and Projected Overexpansion

As a result of demographic and economic pressures, the United States experienced a rapidly increasing participation in higher education during the 1950s and 1960s (see Figure 1-1, p. 2). From a total degree-credit enrollment of 2.10 million in institutions of higher education in 1951, the figure grew to 8.12 million by 1971.[a] The participation rate, measured as a percentage of the population 18 to 24 years of age, was growing from 13.4 percent to 31.6 percent

---

[a]National Center for Educational Statistics, *Digest of Educational Statistics 1972*, table 87, p. 74. These figures refer to the total degree-credit opening fall enrollments of those in first professional, two-year and four-year undergraduate, and four-year resident graduate institutions of higher education.

19

over the same twenty-year period.[2] These trends resulted from a variety of antecedent events. The big postwar birth cohorts enrolled in primary and later secondary schools and greatly increased the demand for college-educated teachers. Then, as the same large cohorts of young people reached college age, the base population of potential students vastly expanded. Government added to the demand for college-educated employees during the post-Sputnik and Vietnam years, when space, defense, and general research and development expenditures were high. Jobs were available for the college educated, and parents and young people alike viewed college education as an avenue for self-improvement, increased earnings, and occupational prestige. Higher education justified the view by providing graduates enhanced opportunities for employment and earnings.

However, there are indications that things are changing and will change even more in the next ten years. Recent Bureau of Labor Statistics reports indicate that by 1985 nearly one worker in five aged 16 years and older will have completed four years of college or more.[3] This has led them to conclude that "it is apparent that one of the major challenges to be met by the economy, both during the current decade and the 1980s, is the continued absorption of this rapidly growing supply of well-educated workers."[4] According to the BLS, by the late 1970s the potential supply will be greater than the potential demand for college graduates in jobs that have traditionally been held by people with this level of education. While college graduates are still expected to hold a competitive employment advantage over those with less education, the problem for them, at least, is going to be increasingly one of job dissatisfaction, underemployment, and lack of job mobility and career opportunity lines. As the Panel on Youth predicts, "This will lead to a new problem, a problem with which the United States has had little experience, the existence of a relatively large group of highly educated but underemployed and disappointed young people."[5]

Supply and demand are the two components that make up the projected overabundance of college-educated workers, and each of these components must be analyzed to assess the size of the potential gap. The implications of the possible existence of such a gap are important, because it suggests an immediate need to influence and redirect young people's career goals at an age prior to entry to college, or to intensify efforts of job creation for the college educated.

Using US Office of Education projections, the Bureau of Labor Statistics has estimated that 20.1 million college level degrees will be awarded during 1972-85 (see Table 2-1). Of the 20.1 million only 13.2 million new graduates will enter the labor force during the period from 1972 to 1985. The remainder represents those entering the Armed Forces or continuing their education, women who marry and don't enter the labor force, and doctorate and master's degree recipients who are employed prior to receiving their advanced degrees and thus are not considered new entrants to the labor force. In addition to the 13.2 million new degree recipients entering the labor market, BLS figures show that

Table 2-1

Projected Number of College Level Degrees to be Awarded in the United States, 1972-85

Degree	Number awarded from 1972-85 (millions)	Percent increase, 1972-85
Total	20.1	46
Bachelor's	14.6	44
Master's	4.0	41
Doctorate	.6	66
First professional	.9	85

Source: Neal H. Rosenthal, "Projected Changes in Occupations," *Monthly Labor Review*, December 1973, p. 22.

an additional 2.1 million persons with a college education will also enter the labor force during 1972-85. This group is made up of 1.2 million persons entering after separation from the military and 0.9 million immigrants, delayed entrants and re-entrants. The components of the total projected supply are outlined below in Table 2-2. In summary, then, it is projected that approximately 15.3 million new college graduates will enter the labor force during 1972-85. It is important here to keep in mind that this is based on an assumed continuation of past enrollment trends. Consequences of alternative projections will be commented upon later.

Table 2-2

Projected Supply of College Graduates to the United States Labor Force, 1972-85

[In thousands]

Source of entrants	1972-85	1972-80	1980-85
Total	15,250	8,850	6,400
New college graduates	13,170	7,540	5,630
Bachelor's	11,200	6,405	4,795
Master's	1,220	700	520
Doctor's	20	10	10
First professional	750	425	325
Military separations	1,150	750	400
Others	910	560	350

Source: Neal H. Rosenthal, "Projected Changes in Occupations," *Monthly Labor Review* December 1973, p. 23.

Demand for college-educated workers comes from growth and upgrading in current jobs, rising credential preferences, and replacement of present college-educated workers who retire or die. The demand arising from occupational growth has to be considered within the context of US economic growth in the future. Here the BLS projects a rather sharp slowdown in economic growth, expected to start about 1978 and continue into the 1980s. The BLS basis for this is given in the statement: "The expected dampening in the rate of economic growth is almost entirely demographic; that is, caused by changes in the growth of the population 16 and over from which the work force is drawn."[6]

To see how the basis for slowing population growth arises it is helpful to look at past and projected births. In Figure 2-1 the number of births from 1930-72 are plotted and the graph is continued to the year 2000 with Bureau of Census projections.[b] Basically four trends can be observed in the graph. From 1937 to 1957 births generally rose—the "baby boom." After a short, relatively stable period from 1957-61, there was a falling trend in the number of births from 1962-73. From 1974-85 births are projected to rise again. This will result from the increased number of women entering childbearing years from earlier large

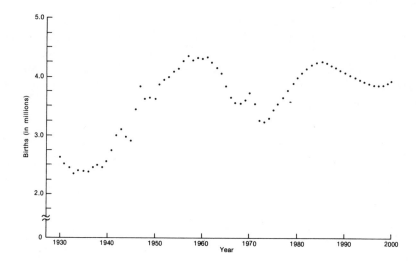

Figure 2-1: Estimated Births in the United States Including Armed Forces Overseas, Calendar Years 1930-72, and Projected for Fiscal Years 1972-73 to 1999-2000. Source: U.S. Bureau of the Census, *Current Population Reports*, Series P-25, No. 499, table 1 and Appendix B. Ibid., No. 493, table 1, Series E.

---

[b]US Bureau of the Census, *Current Population Reports*, Series P-25, No. 493, p. 12. The graph is extended to the year 2000 using Series E, which assumes a replacement total fertility rate of 2.1 births per woman over her childbearing years.

birth cohorts—a secondary effect of the baby boom. Beyond 1985 births are projected to fall once again as the decreasing number of female births between 1962 and 1973 begins to affect the total number of women entering into childbearing years.

Figure 2-1 illustrates the cyclical nature of actual birth patterns in the past and a similar pattern projected for the future. However, the amplitude of the cycles is decreasing with time. This dampening effect with time is the result of the extraordinary decline in fertility rates within the United States. Fertility rates, measured as the number of births per woman during childbearing years, are illustrated in Figure 2-2. From the graph it is observable that fertility rates in the United States have generally been falling since 1957. The dampening of the cyclical nature of the number of births is but one effect of the declining fertility rates, which in turn will lead to declining population growth in the United States.[c]

The trends observable in Figure 2-1 can be used to construct Table 2-3, which relates trends in births to consequences for various societal variables. For primary- and secondary-education levels, where enrollment is close to 100 percent of the population in the age group, the trends in births are an accurate

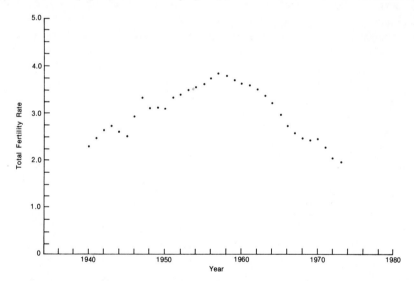

Figure 2-2: Total Fertility Rates in the United States, 1940-73. Source: U.S. Bureau of the Census, *Current Population Reports*, Series P-25, No. 521, May 1974, table B.

[c]Assuming no immigration and a total fertility rate of 2.11, the United States population would stabilize at approximately 270 million by 2030. For additional information, see US Bureau of the Census, *Current Population Reports*, Series P-25, No. 480. It should be noted that the 1973 fertility rate was 1.9.

Table 2-3
Trends in United States Population Bases for Various Societal Variables

Societal Variable	Consequences due to birth trends	
	Generally rising base populations	Generally declining base populations
Entry to elementary school at age 6	1941-67, 1981-91	1968-80, 1992-2003
Entry to secondary school at age 14	1949-75, 1989-99	1976-88, 2000-2011
Entry to labor force at age 16	1951-77, 1991-2001	1978-90, 2002-2013
Entry to college at age 18	1953-79, 1993-2003	1980-92, 2004-2015

Note: Birth trends are based upon data in two sources:

U.S. Bureau of the Census, *Current Population Reports*, Series P-25, No. 499, table 1 and Appendix B.

Ibid., No. 493, table 1, Series E.

precursor of trends in enrollment. It is possible to say with a good deal of assurance that elementary-school enrollments of six-year olds will fall from approximately 1968 to 1980, for example. If the object is to forecast total elementary-school enrollments for grades 1-8 (ages 6-13), analysis of Figure 2-1 shows a high probability that these enrollments will decrease until 1979; and this decrease may continue until 1981 or 1982, depending upon the number of births in the mid-1970s.

As Table 2-3 shows, a falling trend in the number of those available to enter the labor force at age 16 will appear in the period 1978-90. Because of the decreasing number of people reaching 16 years of age between 1978 and 1990 and assuming normal worker retirement and death rates, the growth rate of the labor force 16 and over will also decrease. More specifically, from an expected annual labor-force growth of 1.8 percent over the period 1968-80, the annual growth rate is expected to fall to 1.1 percent during 1980-85.[7] Given a continuation in the long-run declines in average annual hours of work and the long-run increases in labor productivity, the decrease in rates of growth of the labor force result in a projected increase in real GNP of only 3.2 percent a year from 1980-85, as opposed to 4.0 percent during 1968-80.[8]

Based on the projected slowing economic growth, the BLS has estimated the following demand patterns for college graduates as shown in Table 2-4. Comparisons of Tables 2-2 and 2-4 show that the projected oversupply of college graduates is estimated at 50,000 during 1972-80 and at 700,000 during 1980-85. This second figure is particularly alarming because it means an average over-supply of 140,000 new college graduates a year. If this indeed occurs, then

Table 2-4

Projected Demand for College-Educated Workers in the United States, 1972-85

(in millions)

	1972-85	1972-80	1980-85
Total	14.5	8.8	5.7
Growth	7.7	5.0	2.7
Replacements	6.8	3.8	3.0

Source: Neal H. Rosenthal, "Projected Changes in Occupations," *Monthly Labor Review*, December 1973, p. 24.

underemployment and job dissatisfaction are likely to afflict the new college graduates entering the work force. Again no major change in current and past patterns of full-time college attendance is foreseen. This assumption, however, requires closer examination. Continuation of the pattern in the face of low payoff in employment is unlikely.

Some Conclusions

The purpose of this section has been to examine a number of key variables and basic trends. Simple demographic information yielded from past births and falling birth rates suggests trends that can be used to forecast future impact upon various educational and labor force variables. A more detailed exploration of the data will provide background for evaluating Bureau of Labor Statistics forecasts of the economy to 1985. These basic projections provide a basis for forecasting more specific labor-force characteristics such as educational attainment levels and age and sex structures. The projections provide the most extensive and the most current of all forecasts available to those concerned with future employment directed education.

The next section of this chapter will attempt a systematic exploration of the demographic, economic, and social lineaments of the education and employment situation over the next fifteen years. The basic data and information come from US Bureau of Census and Bureau of Labor Statistics reports, but some reanalysis of the data is necessary. An attempt is then made to explore the needs of the employee and employer groups that are deducible from the demographic, economic, and social context traced in the forecasts. The analysis concludes with a brief discussion of resources available to respond to the needs, based on currently available resources and estimates of resources that might be available as the growth of the economy slows over the next fifteen years.

The Demographic, Economic, and Social
Lineaments in Fifteen-Year Perspective

Population

Age Structure. Based upon a projected fertility rate of 2.1 births per woman in childbearing years, Table 2-5 shows the total US population for selected years, both past and projected. The table indicates that even with a fertility rate equal to the replacement rate (2.1), i.e., births replacing deaths and migration effect negligible, the US population will still increase to some 246.6 million people by 1990.

Table 2-5 also reveals some important structural changes in the population as the relative numbers in various age groups shift. Affected by recent large changes in births and fertility, the US age structure has been a continuously changing one. As those born in the baby-boom years advance in age, the cohort bulge runs through to older age groupings in the population. Births in the following years are smaller and the young population declines in relative but not absolute terms. Other lesser birth fluctuations appear, but to a decreased degree.

Table 2-6 shows explicitly the expected changes in the age structure of the population. The 16-and-under age group declines in percentage terms and in absolute numbers from 1972-80, but begins to rise again in numbers during 1980-90. In these years it stays about the same in percentage terms because numbers increase in the 16+ age groups. The 16-19 group increases slightly until 1980, then declines in absolute numbers and in relative terms until 1990. Those 20-34 years will increase by almost 15.5 million during 1972-85 but thereafter the relative size of the group begins to decline and the bulge is picked up by the next age grouping 35-54, which will grow steadily in numbers all during the period. Finally the age group of those 55 and older will increase steadily in numbers all during the period. The largest percentage and absolute gains occur in the 20-34 and 55-and-older age groups during 1972-80, and in the 35-54-year group during 1980-90, while a large loss occurs in the 16-19-year group during 1980-85. The big birth cohorts of postwar years have passed into adult age groups of prime working years. This suggests that work-related education programs will need to be directed at problems that people in the age range 24-54 would be expected to have, and less at the problems of youth.

Sex Structure. Over the next fifteen years the sex structure of the work force will depend on trends that have resulted from recent changes in role definition of women. Women seek greater equality with men in occupational and educational opportunities, participate more fully in the economy as members of the labor force, and bear fewer children. While most of these interesting and important considerations resulting from participation of women in the work force and education will be addressed later, this particular section will elaborate somewhat on the changing fertility patterns of recent times.

Fertility rates have fallen rapidly in the United States, and the two-child family now seems to be the mode of the future. According to a survey done by the US Bureau of Census in June 1973, 70.2 percent of the white wives 18-24 years old expect to have two or fewer children during their childbearing years.[9] To the extent that birth expectations of young wives can be considered harbingers of future births, it appears that the fertility rates will remain low. The time series data in Table 2-7 also illustrates that among all races, the expectation of total births among all age groupings of wives has been decreasing. Thus to the extent that declining fertility rates and birth expectations mean increased participation of women in the labor force, there are grounds to expect a continuation of past trends, and in the future women will increase participation rates and enter new occupations and careers. The problem is to assess the extent to which fertility rates will continue to drop. Some forecasts, such as those of the BLS, assume that fertility rates have dropped about as far as they will, and thus project only slightly increased participation by women in the labor force of the future. It is equally likely that continued low fertility rates will be accompanied by increased employment opportunities for women. If this happens there will not only be an increased rate of female participation in the overall labor force, there will also be changes in the occupational and sectoral structure of female employment. New fields of work will open, and these will require new forms of recruitment, preparation, and selection of women workers. Enrollment structures in schools and training institutions will also change, and differential wages and earnings based on sex must too. With near parity or even a majority of participation in some fields, the future is likely to be very much different for male students and workers.

Ethnic Structure. The population projections outlined above do not include projections by race. The most recent population projections by race undertaken by the US Bureau of Census was done in 1967.[10] Because the fertility rates are not comparable between those used in the projections in 1967 and the more recent projections outlined above, the data are not really useful for comparative predictive purposes. However, the following table (Table 2-8) illustrates some broad racial/age structures in the United States in 1973.

In Figure 2-3 fertility rates are plotted by race since 1940. While the observable trends are comparable, it is obvious that nonwhites have traditionally had higher fertility rates than whites. This has resulted, as shown in Table 2-8, in an increasing percentage of nonwhites in the younger age groups. However, as Figure 2-3 indicates, fertility rates for whites and nonwhites have been slowly moving closer, although there is still a gap between them. The data in Table 2-7 showing birth expectations by race suggest that the trend toward more uniform fertility rates among the races will continue. For example, it shows that while young white wives 18-24 years old have traditionally expressed the lowest expectations of births, young black wives 18-24 years old now express almost identical birth expectations. This suggests that in the long-range future the

Table 2-5
Total Population of the United States, by Age and Sex, July 1, 1972 and Projected to 1980, 1985, and 1990

Sex and age	Number (in thousands)				Percent distribution			
	1972	1980	1985	1990	1972	1980	1985	1990
Both Sexes								
Total, all ages	208,839	224,134	235,699	246,639	100.0	100.0	100.0	100.0
Under 16 years	60,926	56,794	59,979	63,561	29.2	25.3	25.4	25.8
16 years and over	147,913	167,340	175,720	183,078	70.8	74.7	74.6	74.2
16-19 years	15,923	16,397	14,049	13,821	7.6	7.3	6.0	5.6
20-34 years	45,573	58,030	61,195	59,612	21.8	25.9	26.0	24.2
35-54 years	46,365	47,777	53,187	61,519	22.2	21.3	22.6	24.9
55 years and over	40,052	45,136	47,289	48,126	19.2	20.1	20.1	19.5
Men								
Total, all ages	102,053	109,240	114,915	120,376	48.9	48.7	48.8	48.8
Under 16 years	31,055	28,979	30,632	32,465	14.9	12.9	13.0	13.2
16 years and over	70,998	80,261	84,283	87,911	34.0	35.8	35.8	35.6
16-19 years	8,100	8,339	7,139	7,045	3.9	3.7	3.0	2.9
20-34 years	22,740	29,187	30,845	30,061	10.9	13.0	13.1	12.2
35-54 years	22,497	23,249	26,039	30,300	10.8	10.4	11.0	12.3
55 years and over	17,661	19,486	20,260	20,505	8.4	8.7	8.6	8.3

Women								
Total, all ages	106,786	114,894	120,784	126,263	51.1	51.3	51.2	51.2
Under 16 years	29,871	27,815	29,347	31,096	14.3	12.4	12.4	12.6
16 years and over	76,915	87,079	91,437	95,167	36.8	38.8	38.8	38.6
16-19 years	7,823	8,058	6,910	6,776	3.7	3.6	2.9	2.7
20-34 years	22,833	28,843	30,350	29,551	10.9	12.9	12.9	12.0
35-54 years	23,868	24,528	27,148	31,219	11.4	10.9	11.5	12.7
55 years and over	22,391	25,650	27,029	27,621	10.7	11.4	11.5	11.2

Sources: Adapted from Johnston, "Population and Labor Force Projections," *Monthly Labor Review*, December 1973, p. 9, and Johnston, "The US Labor Force: Projections to 1990," *Monthly Labor Review*, July 1973, p. 4.

Table 2-6
Projected Population Changes in the United States, 1972-80, 1980-85, and 1985-90

Age	Change (in thousands)				Percent Change			
	1972-80	1980-85	1985-90	Total 1972-90	1972-80	1980-85	1985-90	Total 1972-90
Total, all ages	15,295	11,565	10,940	37,800	7.3	5.2	4.6	18.1
Under 16	−4,132	3,185	3,582	2,635	−6.8	5.6	6.0	4.3
16 & over	19,427	8,380	7,358	35,165	13.1	5.0	4.2	23.8
16-19 years	474	−2,348	−228	−2,102	3.0	−14.3	−1.6	−13.2
20-34 years	12,457	3,165	−1,583	14,039	27.3	5.5	−2.6	30.8
35-54 years	1,412	5,410	8,332	15,154	3.0	11.3	15.7	32.7
55 and over	5,084	2,153	837	8,074	12.7	4.8	1.8	20.2

Source: See Table 2-5.

Table 2-7
Total Births Expected in the United States, by Age—by Race and Spanish Origin for June 1973, Race for June 1971, and All Races for February-March 1967

(Numbers in thousands. Data limited to currently married women reporting on birth expectations. Civilian noninstitutional population)

Subject	All races			White		Negro		Spanish origin 1973
	1973	1971	1967	1973	1971	1973	1971	
Total Births Expected Per 1,000 Wives								
Total, 14 to 39 years	2,635	2,776	3,115	2,604	2,732	3,015	3,304	3,174
14 to 17 years	2,285	2,491	(B)	2,245	2,417	(B)	(B)	(B)
18 to 24 years	2,262	2,375	2,852	2,262	2,353	2,256	2,623	2,582
18 and 19 years	2,267	2,256	2,719	2,254	2,264	(B)	(B)	(B)
20 and 21 years	2,276	2,373	2,916	2,281	2,368	2,176	2,444	(B)
22 to 24 years	2,254	2,404	2,856	2,255	2,367	2,243	2,787	2,472
25 to 29 years	2,387	2,619	3,037	2,352	2,577	2,799	3,112	2,881
30 to 34 years	2,804	2,989	3,288	2,762	2,936	3,332	3,714	3,784
35 to 39 years	3,234	3,257	3,300	3,180	3,189	3,933	4,223	3,720

Note: (B) Base less than 75,000.
Source: U.S. Bureau of the Census, *Current Population Reports*, Series P-20, No. 265, June 1974, p. 17.

Table 2-8
Estimates of the Total Population of the United States by Age and Race: July 1973 (includes Armed Forces Overseas)

[In thousands]

Age Groups	Population				
	Total	White		Negro & Other	
		Number	Percent of Age Group	Number	Percent of Age Group
All ages	210,404	183,517	87.2	26,887	12.8
Under 16 years	59,941	50,470	84.2	9,471	15.8
16 years & older	150,463	133,047	88.4	17,416	11.6
16-19 years	16,308	13,931	85.4	2,375	14.6
20-34 years	46,936	40,919	87.2	6,017	12.8
35-54 years	46,621	41,294	88.6	5,327	11.4
55 and over	40,599	36,903	90.9	3,695	9.1

Source: U.S. Bureau of the Census, *Current Population Reports*, Series P-25, No. 519, April 1974, p. 12.

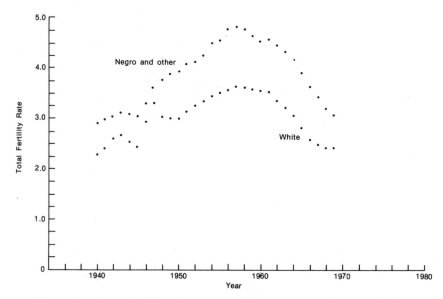

Figure 2-3: Total Fertility Rates in the United States by Race, 1940-69. Source: National Center for Health Statistics, *Vital Statistics of the United States, 1968; Vol. I–Natality*, table 1-6. National Center for Health Statistics, *Vital Statistics of the United States, 1969; Vol. I–Natality*, table 1-6.

disparity in racial fertility rates will disappear, thus eliminating the differential growth rates among races. However, for the time perspective involved in this book, it seems certain that nonwhite races will continue to experience higher fertility rates, and thus their numbers will grow more rapidly than whites in the younger age groups.

The Economy

Bureau of Labor Statistics Projections. As indicated, the demographic pressure provided by decreasing birth rates underlies the BLS economic projections to 1985. As fewer people reach 16 and become eligible to enter the work force, the economic rate of growth is expected to increase less rapidly. After projecting the labor force, assuming a 4 percent unemployment rate, and a continuation of the long-term decreases in hours/week of work and increases in output per man-hour, the BLS is able to project the gross national product for the country. This is expected to total $1.94 trillion by 1985. A macroeconomic model is then used to distribute the GNP into major categories of demand, which in turn is converted into industry employment and finally into occupational needs.[d] Table 2-9 shows the gross national product is projected to grow at 3.2 percent a year from 1980 to 1985, as opposed to 4.6 percent per annum during 1972-80. A general slowing of average annual growth is expected in the private nonagricultural and state and local government sectors.

The implications for employment that arise from the projected GNP are outlined in Table 2-10. The table indicates an economic slowdown evidenced in the decline in the growth of employment. Between 1972 and 1980 there is expected to be a growth of 16 million jobs, while from 1980-85 the figure projected is 6 million. High growth in employment is forecast in government (mainly state and local), in other services, finance, insurance, and real estate. The growth will be sustained until 1985. Manufacturing and trade are expected to show moderate growth rates in employment during 1972-80, but considerably slower growth from 1980-85. Government and "other services" will provide most of the new employment projected for the slow years beyond 1980. These two fields are expected to account for some 4.3 million of the 6 million additional jobs projected for 1980-85. The sectoral designation "other services" is not directly useful for developing work-related educational policies or programs, inasmuch as it includes both large numbers of jobs for which highly specific technical and professional training will be required, as well as large numbers of jobs for which no specific training is required. The more appropriate place to examine the matter is in the occupational structure of the future work force.

---

[d]For a more detailed statement concerning the assumptions made and the methodology used in the BLS projections, see Jack Alterman, "An Overview of BLS Projections," pp. 3-7.

Table 2-9

Changes in Gross National Product and Productivity in the United States, Selected Years 1955-72 and Projected to 1980 and 1985

Category	Actual				Projected		Average annual rate of growth[a]					
	1955	1960	1968	1972	1980	1985	1955-68	1968-72	1968-85	1968-80	1972-80	1980-85
Total GNP (billions of 1972 dollars)	$645.9	$717.1	$1,038.6	$1,155.2	$1,657.9	$1,942.5	3.72	2.69	3.75	3.97	4.62	3.22
Government	90.7	96.5	134.3	135.4	157.3	174.9	3.07	.20	1.57	1.33	1.89	2.14
Federal	51.9	47.5	61.7	50.3	47.2	47.6	1.34	-4.98	-1.51	-2.21	-.79	.17
Military	28.2	23.5	32.8	22.4	18.7	18.7	1.17	-9.09	-3.25	-4.57	-2.23	.00
Civilian	23.7	24.1	28.8	27.8	28.5	28.9	1.51	-.88	.02	-.09	.31	.28
State and local	38.8	49.0	72.7	85.1	110.1	127.3	4.95	4.02	3.35	3.52	3.27	2.95
Private	555.2	620.6	904.3	1,019.7	1,500.6	1,767.6	3.82	3.05	4.02	4.31	4.95	3.33
Agriculture	29.2	30.6	32.6	34.4	35.3	37.1	.85	1.25	.76	3.67	.33	1.00
Nonagriculture	526.0	590.0	871.7	985.3	1,465.3	1,730.5	3.96	3.11	4.12	4.42	5.09	3.38
Private GNP per man-hour (1972 dollars)	4.36	4.88	6.42	7.04	9.02	10.34	3.02	2.33	2.84	2.87	3.15	2.77
Agriculture	1.83	2.40	3.69	4.40	7.04	9.18	5.54	4.50	5.51	5.53	6.05	5.45
Nonagriculture	4.72	5.15	6.60	7.19	9.09	10.37	2.61	2.16	2.69	2.70	2.97	2.67
Average annual man-hours (private)[b]	2,130	2,067	2,000	1,965	1,920	1,888	-.48	-.44	-.34	-.34	-.29	-.34
Agriculture	2,480	2,366	2,314	2,267	2,180	2,127	-.53	-.51	-.49	-.50	-.49	-.49
Nonagriculture	2,088	2,039	1,982	1,950	1,913	1,883	-.40	-.41	-.30	-.29	-.24	-.32

[a]Compound interest rate between terminal years.
[b]Limited to private because of the concept used to compute productivity and the assumption of no change in hours in government.
Source: Ronald E. Kutscher, "Projections of GNP, Income, Output and Employment," *Monthly Labor Review*, December 1973, p. 28.

Some interesting implications follow from the assumptions underlying the projections. The projected decrease in hours of work assumes a continuation of a trend toward more leisure time for the American worker. In the future, with increasing numbers of people retiring younger from their primary jobs, work-related education programs may have to provide opportunities for these people to expand their skills or retrain for second careers that may grow out of hobbies or avocations into full or part-time employment, either on a paid or a volunteer basis.

The assumption of a 4 percent unemployment rate is based on a further assumption that "fiscal, monetary, and manpower training and educational programs will achieve a satisfactory balance between relatively low unemployment and relative price stability."[11] It is worth pointing out that unemployment is currently over 8 percent, and likely headed upward. Inflation is increasing at 12 percent a year. The current high level of unemployment combined with a high level of inflation results in a situation for which there is little recent experience to guide future employment projections or policies.

Finally, the projected economic slowdown may have implications for education in somewhat broader terms also. A decline in the rate of economic growth means a probable decline in the growth rate of revenues directed into work/education programs in particular, and investments in human resource development in general. In a future of generally decreasing growth in economic activity compounded by a time of relative scarcity in energy or food and abnormal levels of inflation, it is difficult to foresee what attitudes will be reflected in policies and decisions to invest in general education. The need to stimulate economic activity may keep funds flowing at increasing levels to those forms of education and training that are seemingly more closely related to work and production.

Work Force

Demographic Characteristics. The total size and the age and sex structure of the work force will have obvious importance for the future. Table 2-11 shows BLS projections of the labor force and labor-force participation rates until 1990. From a labor force total of almost 86 million in 1970, the US labor force is projected to increase to 112,576,000 in 1990. This increase of nearly 27 million in absolute numbers represents an increase in the participation rate of only slightly more than 1 percent. Slightly more than 60 percent of the population 16 and over were in the work force in 1970, and only slightly more than 61 percent are in the work force in 1990; and this participation rate is moving only very slightly over the thirty-year period from 1960 to 1990. Behind this lies the noticeable feature that the growth of the labor force slows considerably during the 1980s. From an average annual rate of growth of 1.7 percent in the 1970s, the labor-force growth rate is expected to fall to 1.0 percent a year during the

Table 2-10
Total Employment[a] in the United States by Major Industry Sector, 1960, 1972, and Projected to 1980 and 1985

[Numbers in thousands]

Industry sector	Actual		Projected[b]		Percent distribution				Number change			Average annual rate of change[c]		
	1960	1972	1980	1985	1960	1972	1980	1985	1960-72	1972-80	1980-85	1960-72	1972-80	1980-85
Total	68,869	85,597	101,576	107,609	100.0	100.0	100.0	100.0	16,728	15,979	6,033	1.8	2.2	1.2
Government[d]	8,353	13,290	16,610	18,800	12.1	15.5	16.4	17.5	4,937	3,320	2,190	3.9	2.8	2.5
Total private	60,516	72,307	84,966	88,809	87.9	84.5	83.6	82.5	11,791	12,659	3,843	1.5	2.0	.9
Agriculture	5,389	3,450	2,300	1,900	7.8	4.0	2.3	1.8	-1,939	-1,150	-400	-3.7	-4.9	-3.7
Nonagriculture	55,124	68,857	82,666	86,909	80.0	80.4	81.4	80.8	13,733	13,809	4,243	1.8	2.3	1.0
Mining	748	645	655	632	1.1	.8	.6	.6	-103	10	-23	-1.2	1.2	-.7
Contract construction	3,654	4,352	4,908	5,184	5.3	5.1	4.8	4.8	698	556	276	1.4	1.5	1.1
Manufacturing	17,197	19,281	22,923	23,499	25.0	22.5	22.6	21.8	2,084	3,642	576	1.0	2.2	.5
Durable goods	9,681	11,091	13,629	14,154	14.1	13.0	13.4	13.2	1,410	2,538	525	1.1	2.6	.8
Nondurable goods	7,516	8,190	9,294	9,345	10.9	9.6	9.2	8.7	674	1,104	51	.7	1.6	.1
Transportation and public utilities	4,214	4,726	5,321	5,368	6.1	5.5	5.2	5.0	512	595	47	1.1	1.5	.2
Transportation	2,743	2,842	3,250	3,266	4.0	3.3	3.2	3.0	99	408	16	.3	1.7	.1
Communication	844	1,150	1,300	1,312	1.2	1.3	1.3	1.2	306	150	12	2.6	1.5	.2
Public utilities	624	734	771	790	.8	.9	.8	.7	110	47	19	1.4	.8	.5
Wholesale and retail trade	14,177	18,432	21,695	22,381	20.6	21.5	21.4	20.8	4,255	3,263	686	2.2	2.1	.6
Wholesale	3,295	4,235	4,946	5,123	4.8	4.9	4.9	4.8	940	711	177	2.1	2.0	.7
Retail	10,882	14,197	16,749	17,258	15.8	16.6	16.5	16.0	3,315	2,552	509	2.2	2.1	.6

Finance, insurance and real estate	2,985	4,303	5,349	5,932	4.3	5.0	5.3	5.5	1,318	1,046	583	3.0	2.8	2.1
Other services[e]	12,152	17,118	21,815	23,913	17.6	20.0	21.5	22.2	4,966	4,697	2,098	2.8	3.1	1.9

[a]Employment in this table is on a "jobs" rather than a "persons" concept and includes, in addition to wage and salary workers, self-employed and unpaid family workers. Employment on a job concept differs from employment on a person concept by separately counting each job held by a multiple job holder.

[b]Among the assumptions underlying these projections is a 4-percent unemployment rate.

[c]Compound interest rate between terminal years.

[d]Includes domestic wage and salary workers and government enterprise employees; does not include employees paid from nonappropriated funds.

[e]Includes paid household employment.

Source: U.S. Department of Labor, *1974 Manpower Report of the President*, p. 355.

Table 2-11
Total United States Labor Force and Labor-Force-Participation Rates by Age and Sex, 1960 and 1970 and Projected to 1980, 1985, and 1990

(Numbers in thousands)

Sex and Age Group	Total Labor Force					Projected Changes		Participation Rate, in %				
	Actual		Projected					Actual			Projected	
	1960	1970	1980	1985	1990	1970–1980	1980–1990	1960	1970	1980	1985	1990
Both sexes												
Total, 16 and over	72,104	85,903	101,809	107,716	112,576	15,906	10,767	59.2	60.3	60.8	61.3	61.5
16 to 24 years	12,720	19,916	23,781	22,184	20,319	3,865	−3,462	58.4	61.7	63.5	64.5	64.2
25 to 54 years	46,596	51,487	61,944	69,202	76,421	10,457	14,477	68.8	71.7	73.1	73.6	74.0
55 years and over	12,788	14,500	16,084	16,330	15,836	1,584	−248	39.6	37.8	35.6	34.5	32.9
Men												
Total, 16 and over	48,933	54,343	62,590	66,017	68,907	8,247	6,317	82.4	79.2	78.0	78.3	78.4
16 to 19 years	3,162	4,395	4,668	3,962	3,901	273	−767	58.6	57.5	56.0	55.5	55.4
20 to 24 years	4,939	7,378	8,852	8,496	7,404	1,474	−1,448	88.9	85.1	83.0	82.5	82.1
25 to 34 years	10,940	11,974	17,523	19,400	19,853	5,549	2,330	96.4	95.0	94.6	94.4	94.4
35 to 44 years	11,454	10,818	11,851	14,617	17,398	1,033	5,547	96.4	95.7	95.1	94.9	94.7
45 to 54 years	9,568	10,487	9,908	9,744	10,909	−579	1,001	94.3	92.9	91.9	91.7	91.5
55 to 64 years	6,445	7,127	7,730	7,716	7,307	603	−423	85.2	81.5	79.1	78.1	77.5
65 years and over	2,425	2,164	2,058	2,082	2,135	−106	77	32.2	25.8	21.2	20.0	19.3

Women

Total, 16 and over	23,171	31,560	39,219	41,699	43,669	7,659	4,450	37.1	42.8	45.0	45.6	45.9
16 to 19 years	2,061	3,250	3,669	3,203	3,188	419	−481	39.1	43.7	45.5	46.4	47.0
20 to 24 years	2,558	4,893	6,592	6,523	5,826	1,699	−766	46.1	57.5	63.4	64.9	66.2
25 to 34 years	4,159	5,704	9,256	10,339	10,678	3,552	1,422	35.8	44.8	50.2	50.9	51.5
35 to 44 years	5,325	5,971	6,369	8,560	10,219	398	3,850	43.1	50.9	53.2	54.4	55.2
45 to 54 years	5,150	6,533	6,537	6,542	7,364	4	827	49.3	54.0	56.2	57.4	58.0
55 to 64 years	2,964	4,153	5,057	5,213	5,003	904	−54	36.7	42.5	44.7	45.4	45.8
65 years and over	954	1,056	1,239	1,319	1,391	183	152	10.5	9.2	8.6	8.5	8.3

Source: Denis F. Johnston, "The U.S. Labor Force: Projections to 1990," *Monthly Labor Review*, July 1973, p. 4.

1980s. Changes in the age and sex structures of the future labor force add important detail to the projections of slower labor-force growth, and are summarized in the following items.

1. The teenage labor force is expected to increase less rapidly during the 1970s than during the 1960s, and is expected to decrease in numbers during the 1980s.
2. The 20-24 age group is expected to grow rapidly during the remainder of the 1970s but to decline by 2.2 million during the 1980s.
3. The largest increases in any age bracket occur in the 25-34-year-old group, which will increase by some 9.1 million in the 1970s and by another 3.8 million in the 1980s.
4. The 35-44 age group will be greatly increased in the 1980s, again as a result of the aging of cohorts born in the baby-boom years.
5. Those 45-64 years old are expected to increase by almost 2.3 million by 1990.
6. Those older than 65 are expected to increase moderately until 1990.
7. The male labor force participation rate is expected to decline slightly between 1970 and 1990, but the total numbers will increase by 14.6 million to a total of 68.9 million.
8. By 1990 the women's labor force is expected to increase by 12.1 million over the 1970 figure of 31.6 million. Women of all age groups, except those over 65, are expected to continue their growth in participation rates, although at a considerably lessened pace than during the 1960s and 1970s. This is a result of BLS assumptions that fertility rates will not continue their downward plunge but will tend to level off at approximately the replacement rate. It should be noted that if a fertility rate of 1.8 instead of 2.1 is assumed in the projections, an additional 500,000 women will be available to join the labor force in 1985.[12] The additional increase arises from women released from childbearing responsibilities.
9. There is not much change in the sex distribution of the labor force predicted. In 1970 men comprised 63.3 percent of the labor force, and by 1990 this is expected to decline to 61.2 percent.

Occupational Structure. While the major economic sectors in which job growth will occur in the future have already been outlined, projected growth in occupations will have more direct relevance for shaping work-related education policies. Projections indicate that the greatest growth—approximately 15 million jobs—will occur in the white-collar occupations. An actual decrease in jobs for farmworkers is expected (see Table 2-12). This follows a trend of actual decrease in employment in agriculture between 1969 and 1972. It assumes that the present technology and large-scale organization of agricultural production will continue to grow in the United States. With changes in energy supplies and declining employment in other sectors this may not be realistic, and smaller and

Table 2-12
Employment in the United States by Occupation Group, 1972, and Projected 1980 and 1985 Requirements

[Numbers in thousands]

Occupation group	Actual 1972		Projected 1980[a]		Projected 1985[a]		Number change		Average annual rate of change[b]	
	Number	Percent distribution	Number	Percent distribution	Number	Percent distribution	1972-80	1980-85	1972-80	1980-85
Total employment[c]	81,703	100.0	95,800	100.0	101,500	100.0	14,097	5,700	20.0	1.2
Professional and technical workers	11,459	14.0	15,000	15.7	17,000	16.8	3,541	2,000	3.5	2.5
Managers and administrators, except farm	8,032	9.8	10,100	10.5	10,500	10.3	2,068	400	2.8	.8
Sales workers	5,354	6.6	6,300	6.6	6,500	6.4	946	200	2.1	.5
Clerical workers	14,247	17.4	17,900	18.7	19,700	19.4	3,653	1,800	2.9	1.9
Craft and kindred workers	10,810	13.2	12,300	12.8	13,000	12.8	1,490	700	1.6	1.2
Operatives	13,549	16.6	15,000	15.6	15,300	15.1	1,451	300	1.6	.5
Nonfarm laborers	4,217	5.2	4,500	4.7	4,500	4.4	283	0	.7	0
Service workers	10,966	13.4	12,700	13.3	13,400	13.2	1,734	700	1.9	1.0
Farmers and farm laborers	3,069	3.8	2,000	2.1	1,600	1.6	-1,069	-400	-5.4	-4.4

[a]Among the assumptions underlying these projections is a 4-percent unemployment rate.
[b]Compound interest rate between terminal years.
[c]Represents total employment as covered by the Current Population Survey.
Source: U.S. Department of Labor, *1974 Manpower Report of the President*, p. 355.

less productive farming may provide residual employment as it does in many other countries and did in this country until recent times. Hence, this forecast of decrease is not accepted as it stands.

For professional, technical, and clerical workers the average annual rate of growth in new jobs is substantial, even during the years beyond 1980 when the economic slowdown is predicted. The total number of jobs that will be opening up by 1985, however, includes both growth and replacement; hence it is necessary to estimate replacement jobs that will open through retirement or death. The total job openings resultant from growth and replacement during 1972-85 are outlined in Table 2-13. The greatest number of total job openings will occur in the white-collar classification, and this is dominated by the clerical and kindred group, which is expected to total 44 percent of the total 38,800,000 openings for white-collar workers during 1972-85. Blue-collar occupations, on the other hand, will generally result in fewer total openings. In 1972, blue-collar workers comprised 35 percent of the total labor force, yet

Table 2-13
Projected Job Openings[a] in the United States by Major Occupational Group, 1972-85

[In thousands]

Occupational group	Total	Growth	Replacement
Total	61,200	19,800	41,400
White-collar workers	38,800	·14,600	24,200
Professional and technical	12,000	5,600	6,400
Managers, officials, and proprietors	5,900	2,400	3,500
Sales workers	3,800	1,100	2,700
Clerical and kindred	17,000	5,400	11,600
Blue-collar workers	13,800	4,200	9,600
Craftsmen and kindred	5,300	2,200	3,100
Operatives[b]	7,200	1,800	5,500
Nonfarm laborers	1,300	200	1,000
Service workers	8,500	2,400	6,000
Private household workers	700	−400	1,100
Other service workers	7,800	2,800	4,900
Farm workers	50	−1,400	1,400

[a]Resulting from occupational growth and replacement of workers who leave the labor force.
[b]Includes the 1970 census classification, operatives, except transport and transport equipment operatives.
Note: Details may not add to totals because of rounding.
Source: Neal H. Rosenthal, "Projected Changes in Occupations," *Monthly Labor Review*, December 1973, p. 22.

during 1972-85 only 23 percent of the 61.2 million total job openings are expected to be available in these occupations. The large growth in employment forecast for "other services" in the economic activity sectoral forecasts appears under two categories in the occupational forecasts. Jobs requiring professional and technical training appear in the "professional and technical" workers category; and other service jobs requiring less special and advanced training are in the occupational category, "service workers." Though the largest numbers will be "service workers" rather than professional, the job growth for professional and technical workers in services outside government, industry, and other sectors will be quite large. That this possibility is already perceived by present cohorts of students is reflected in the very large demand for entrance to professional schools. Whether institutional policies and programs are responding is not so clear, and with limited places in many of the better schools, the demand will either be shunted off to inferior schools or other fields of study entirely.

Unemployment. BLS projections are based on an assumed 4 percent unemployment rate. While it is not possible to detail any sectoral or occupational structure for future unemployment, recent and partial data may help to identify certain segments of the labor force in need of job training, retraining, guidance, and many other activities linking employment to education. Now, in the first half of 1975, the BLS assumptions of a 4 percent unemployment rate may seem grotesquely out of line with the current unemployment rate, which is hovering near 8 percent, with predictions that it will rise to 10 percent before the end of the year. The difference may seem so great that the analysis based on the 4 percent rate will be useless. Yet the contrary is the case. Even with the 4 percent rate, the future consequences for unemployment or underemployment of educated workers are serious. With the current unemployment the prospects are even bleaker, but assuming that the rate begins to fall in 1976, as forecasters are hoping it will, there will still be a serious problem of providing jobs for educated workers over the next fifteen years. The only difference is one of degree of seriousness.

Recent unemployment figures, categorized by occupation, industry, and other selected labor-force characteristics, show that the really severe present unemployment problems exist for young people 16-19 years of age of both sexes, black and other nonwhite races, and young veterans aged 20-24.[13] Operatives, nonfarm laborers, and service workers and wage and salary workers in construction, wholesale, and retail trade all experienced higher-than-average unemployment rates in 1973.[14]

With past unemployment figures and the industry and occupational growth figures presented earlier, it may be useful to study growth areas in terms of potential unemployment. Tables 2-14 and 2-15 attempt to do this, using average unemployment rates since 1967 by industry and by occupation. To the extent that trends in past unemployment rates will be followed in the future, these

Table 2-14

Past United States Unemployment Rates and Projected Job Openings by Occupation

Occupational Growth Rate, 1972-85[b]	Unemployment rates[a]		
	High > 6.0	Average 3.0-6.0	Low < 3.0
High > 90		Clerical & kindred	Professional & technical
Average 60-89		Sales workers Service workers	Managers & administrators
Low < 60	Operatives; Non-farm laborers	Craftsmen & kindred	Farm workers

[a]An average unemployment rate for the years 1967-73 was calculated for each occupational grouping.

[b]This is a measure of occupational expansion, expressing job openings, by occupation during the period 1972-85, as a percentage of the base employment in that occupation in 1972. Job openings are the result of absolute job growth in an occupation and turnover due to death or retirement.

Note: Average unemployment rates were calculated from the historical unemployment rates by occupation. See U.S. Department of Labor, *1974 Manpower Report of the President*, p. 275. Occupational growth rates, 1972-85 were calculated from data in Tables 2-12 and 2-13.

tables give some indication of future high- and low-growth occupations and industries, and their potential unemployment problems. While the distinction in Tables 2-14 and 2-15 between high, average, and low rates is somewhat arbitrary, the ideal situation would be to have low unemployment accompanying high growth. The worst situation would be to have high unemployment and low growth.

The important points on job growth and replacement in occupations and industries cross-classified by unemployment prospects may be summarized:

1. White-collar workers fare well in all categories, but professional and technical workers are expected to have high growth rates in employment accompanied by low unemployment—a very favorable mix of characteristics.
2. Blue-collar workers, especially operatives and non-farm laborers, will experience low growth rates and relatively high unemployment.
3. Farm workers can be expected to experience low unemployment, but with low growth rates also, while service workers will have average growth and unemployment rates.
4. Government appears in the enviable position of high growth and low unemployment, while wage and salary agriculture stands at the other extreme: high unemployment and low growth.

Table 2-15

Past United States Unemployment Rates and Projected Employment Growth by Industry

	Unemployment Rates[a]		
	High > 6.0	Average 3.5-6.0	Low < 3.5
High > 35		Service industries	Government; Finance, insurance and real estate
Average 15-34	Construction	Manufacturing; Wholesale & retail trade	
Low < 15	Agricultural wage and salary		Mining; Transportation & public utilities

[a]An average unemployment rate for the years 1967-73 was calculated for each industry.

[b]This is a measure of employment expansion, expressing absolute employment growth by industry during the period 1972-85 as a percentage of the total employment in that industry in 1972.

Note: Average unemployment rates were calculated from historical unemployment rates by industry. See U.S. Department of Labor, *1974 Manpower Report of the President*, p. 276. Employment growth rates, 1972-85 were calculated from Table 2-10.

Again for reasons previously discussed, our estimates do not exactly agree with official forecasts for agricultural employment. Though growth in full-time wage employment may be slow failing employment opportunities in other sectors of activity, many workers may move into part-time wage employment in agriculture, or go into small-scale farming at lowered levels of productivity and thus be "self-employed." Establishing true employment status in such a situation is very difficult methodologically; much less is it easy to project the future situation accurately or precisely. This kind of part-time work or low-productivity self-employment in agriculture has more relevance to the need for extension programs and nonformal education to raise productivity.

Educational Attainment. Another characteristic of the labor force that is extremely important when considering training needs is the educational attainment structure of the work force. In all forecasts the labor force is expected to continue its steady increase in educational levels attained. Tables 2-16 and 2-17 show the growth forecast for particular educational attainment levels. The largest percentage changes occur in the group with four or more years of college education and in the group with eight or fewer years of education. The college-graduate group is expected to expand by 138 percent between 1970 and

Table 2-16

United States Civilian Labor Force 16 Years and Older, by Years of School Completed, 1970, and Projected to 1980 and 1990

	Numbers (in millions)			Change 1970-90 (in millions)	% Change
	1970	1980	1990		
Total civilian labor force 16 and over	80.4	99.8	110.6	+30.2	38
Labor force with given education level					
4+ college	10.1	16.4	24.0	+13.9	138
1-3 college	10.6	15.8	20.0	+9.4	89
4 high school	28.2	40.3	44.8	+16.4	58
1-3 high school	17.2	17.3	15.7	−1.5	−9
8 or less	14.4	10.0	6.1	−8.3	−57

Note: Figures may not add to totals because of rounding.

Source: Johnston, "Education of Workers: Projections to 1990," *Monthly Labor Review*, November 1973, p. 24.

Table 2-17

Changes in Educational Attainment 1970-90 for the United States Civilian Labor Force 25 Years and Older

	Percentage of labor force with given education level			
Education	1970-72 average	1980	1985	1990
4+ college	14.6	18.5	21.2	23.8
1-3 college	12.0	14.0	15.2	16.4
4 high school	37.5	40.7	41.3	41.2
1-3 high school	16.9	15.1	13.8	12.5
8 or less	19.0	11.8	8.5	6.1

Source: Johnston, "Education of Workers: Projections to 1990," *Monthly Labor Review* November 1973, p. 23.

1990; the group with eight or fewer years of education is expected to decrease by 57 percent over the same period. The projected increase in educational attainment will result from an increase in the number of relatively well-educated young people who enter the work force to replace relatively less-educated older workers who retire. This is shown clearly in Table 2-18.

The projected upgrading of educational levels for the civilian labor force has some important implications. We have already seen that the BLS is predicting an oversupply of some 700,000 college graduates during 1980-85. This does not mean 700,000 unemployed college-educated people. Rather it means these

Table 2-18
Projected Percentage of Specific Age Groups with Given Education Levels, for the United States Civilian Labor Force 1980 and 1990

Year	Education level	Age							
		16&17	18&19	20-24	25-34	35-44	45-54	55-64	65+
1980	4+ college	—	0.1	14.6	24.1	18.8	15.1	12.1	13.5
	1-3 college	0.1	13.4	30.5	17.6	13.9	11.3	11.1	9.0
	4 high school	2.0	55.5	42.3	42.2	42.9	40.1	39.4	25.6
	1-3 high school	92.0	27.2	8.6	11.9	16.0	17.5	17.4	14.5
	8 or less	5.9	3.8	4.0	4.1	8.4	15.9	20.0	37.4
1990	4+ college	—	0.1	18.3	29.7	24.9	19.0	16.1	16.4
	1-3 college	0.1	14.0	35.7	19.7	17.0	14.2	11.9	10.6
	4 high school	1.9	57.9	38.0	39.8	41.8	43.5	41.6	34.8
	1-3 high school	93.8	25.5	5.3	8.8	12.4	15.6	16.5	15.0
	8 or less	4.2	2.4	2.7	2.0	3.7	7.7	14.0	23.3

Source: Johnston, "Education of Workers: Projections to 1990," *Monthly Labor Review*, November 1973, pp. 25-26.

college-educated workers will be competing—probably successfully—with less-educated workers, and replacing them in jobs that have traditionally been held by noncollege graduates. This, in turn, assumes continued rising job-entry requirements and an increased emphasis on credentials. The result of this may be increased job dissatisfaction for many college graduates who find themselves underemployed in work that is below their level of expectation. It may also mean increased unemployment problems for the less-educated and unskilled workers of the United States.[e]

In actual fact, however, the oversupply of college graduates that has been forecast may not appear. There are a number of recent indications that college enrollments may not continue the same growth trends that led to the enormous expansion in higher education of the 1950s and 1960s. As one indicator, the proportion of high-school seniors enrolled in college in the fall of the year of their graduation has fallen from its high of 55 percent in 1968 to 49 percent in 1972.[15] First-time enrollments for degree-credit in institutions of higher education also fell, from 1,780,000 in 1970 to 1,738,000 in 1972.[16] The rate of growth of young people who graduate from high school is slowing, and by 1990 it is expected that some 92 percent of those 20-24 years old will have received a high-school diploma.[17] As this growth rate slows, the growth of potential college enrollments among the young must also slow. In fact, as reported in the Second Newman Report, the average annual rate of increase in college enrollments was 8.2 percent during the 1960s, but by 1972 it was 1.9 percent.[18] The Office of Education states that "we now seem to be in the midst of changing enrollment patterns in post-secondary education."[19]

Although these are short-term trends, the above figures suggest that the projected oversupply of highly educated manpower may be inflated. While this may relieve the oversupply problem, it aggravates the institutional situation for colleges and universities that have expanded and overexpanded during the boom years of higher education. As Table 2-3 (p. 24) indicates, the slowing in the growth of college enrollments has come at a time when the base population from which colleges usually draw their students is still increasing. The number of people eighteen years old is expected to increase until 1979 before declining. Beginning about 1980 there will be no further demographic impetus to continued growth in college and university enrollments, and the growth will have to occur largely through increased participation rates. If in the traditional college age group—18-24 years old—demand for a higher education is slowing, one alternative is for colleges to increase participation rates among the older people in this country.

The Carnegie Commission on Higher Education and the US Bureau of Census have both published enrollment projections showing a considerably decreased

[e]In times of economic "stagnation" like the present, college graduates in New York City are even competing with the poor for jobs. See Michael Stern, "College Graduates Vying with Poor for Jobs Here," *New York Times*, November 20, 1974, p. 1.

growth in higher education. Subsequent to the publication of the BLS projection of a college-educated oversupply problem, the US Office of Education has also published enrollment projections that have been revised downward considerably from the previous OE figures that the Bureau of Labor Statistics used in making their projections.[20] Table 2-19 illustrates the range of available enrollment projections.

A comparison of the previous and the latest Office of Education projections of earned degrees shows that for the years during the early 1980s that are included in the projections, the BLS gap of 140,000 excess college graduates per year is eliminated.[f] Thus it seems fair to question the oversupply projected. It is possible that a general gap may not exist. It is more likely that there will continue to be specific areas of oversupply rather than the predicted general oversupply. This is not to argue that the problem is not still a serious one, either for the college graduates in these years, or for the less educated with whom they will be competing for employment.

Women in the Work Force. Recent *Monthly Labor Review* reports indicate that in the past, women as well as men have found jobs in the fastest-growing industries—services, government, trade, and manufacturing.[21] Services is the largest employer of women. In the service occupations approximately 11.4 million, or 63 percent of all employees, in 1970 were women. Most of these women are employed in the professional services of health, medicine, and education. However, manufacturing and trade also employ over 5.5 million women each, and comprise the next two largest employers of women.

While women have found employment in the fast-growing industries, they have remained grouped within only a few occupations.[22] In fact over 54 percent of all employed women work as clerical and kindred or services workers (except private household), while another 15 percent work as operatives. Men and women are fairly evenly distributed by percentages in the professional and technical and sales areas, but women are underrepresented as managers and administrators. Even in the service enterprises, in which women predominate, women are underrepresented as managers and administrators. Although 51 percent more women than men were employed in services in 1970, only 28 percent of the managers and administrators were women.[23]

The data for women employed in nonagricultural industries classified by educational attainment levels is also interesting. Whereas women with a high-

[f]Compare US Office of Education, *Projections of Educational Statistics to 1982-83* table 21, p. 46 and US Office of Education, *Projections of Educational Statistics to 1981-82*, table 21, p. 48. For example the latest OE figures project that a total of 1,446,800 college level degrees (undergraduate, graduate, and first professional) will be awarded in 1981. The similar earlier Office of Education figure that was used by the Bureau of Labor Statistics was 1,679,400. The difference between the two OE projections is well in excess of the BLS projected college oversupply gap of 140,000 per year, even after making allowance for the fact that there will be some college graduates who will not enter the labor market.

Table 2-19

Alternative Projected Total Degree and Nondegree Credit Enrollment in All Institutions of Higher Education[a] in the United States, 1970-90

(In thousands)

Fall of year	Actual	U.S. Office of Education (1974)	U.S. Office of Education (1973)	Carnegie Commission Projection II	U.S. Bureau of the Census, Series E-2
1970	8,581	8,581	8,581	8,649	—
1971	8,949	8,949	8,949	—	—
1972	9,215	9,215	9,124	—	—
1973		9,385	9,675	—	—
1974		9,568	10,117	—	—
1975		9,802	10,562	—	9,147
1976		10,034	10,977	—	—
1977		10,242	11,369	—	—
1978		10,406	11,722	—	—
1979		10,485	12,023	—	—
1980		10,517	12,293	11,446	10,284
1981		10,516	12,532	—	—
1982		10,416	—	—	—
.		.	.	.	
1985		—	—	10,555	10,207
.		.	.	.	
1990		—	—	—	10,397

[a]This includes resident and extension, 4-year and 2-year institutions of higher education.

Sources: U.S. Office of Education, *Projections of Educational Statistics to 1981-82*, p. 23; U.S. Office of Education, *Projections of Educational Statistics to 1982-83*, p. 24; U.S. Bureau of Census, *Current Population Reports*, Series P-25, No. 476, p. 19; Carnegie Commission on Higher Education, *Priorities for Action: Final Report of the Carnegie Commission on Higher Education*, New York: McGraw-Hill, 1973, p. 100.

school education or less are fairly evenly distributed among manufacturing, trade, and service, once a woman has any college training, the percentage employed in the various industries begins to shift heavily towards the service field.[24] Of women college graduates or those with advanced training, a full 80 percent are employed in the services, most of them, obviously, in the professional service fields of education and health. While men with advanced degrees show a similar shift toward service, the percentage (44 percent) is not nearly so large. Thus it seems likely that as women continue approaching greater equality of opportunity with men, the representation of college-educated women in non-service industries will increase.

Some Conclusions. There are a number of points concerning the future labor force that are important when considering future needs for education/employment programs.

1. The labor force will expand by 26.7 million until the projected figure of 112.6 million workers is reached in 1990.

2. There will be decreasing numbers in the teenage labor force (16-19 years old) during the 1980s, thus suggesting less pressure in addressing the high unemployment and lack of skills characteristic in this age range.

3. There will be large increases in the number of workers aged 25-34 throughout the period 1970-90. Educational programs will increasingly need to focus on problems of job redesign to reduce job dissatisfaction and use of leisure time, since this age group is largely employed or have home responsibilities. Similar needs will be felt throughout the 1980s in the 35-44 age group. To the extent that there are decreasing numbers of young workers and increasing numbers of workers aged 25-44, education/employment programs will need increasingly to shift emphasis from entry-level training to programs designed to meet the needs of the already established worker.

4. Men of all ages are expected to have lower participation rates in the work force, whereas women will increase their participation rates. However, the BLS expects the rapid expansion of female labor-force participation to slow as fertility rates stop their rapid decline of recent years. The nature of future fertility patterns is an important indicator of labor-force participation.

5. Women can be expected to shift from those relatively few occupations in which they are employed to occupational patterns which are more diversified. One area of potentially increased employability is as managers and administrators.

6. There are expected to be 61,200,000 job openings that will result from growth and replacement during 1972-85. Fully 63 percent of these will occur in the white-collar area. The largest growth of new jobs will occur in the professional and technical area, but because of the large number of replacements needed in clerical occupations, the largest total job openings will be experienced in that area.

7. When past unemployment trends are used as an indication of potential future unemployment, white-collar occupations of all kinds are expected to experience average or better growth accompanied by average or lower unemployment. Blue-collar occupations are expected to have low growth rates of employment, with accompanying average or higher rates of unemployment.

8. Wage and salary agriculture is the only employment field in which high future unemployment is likely to accompany the low growth in jobs expected to occur according to BLS projections. This does not mean that substantial numbers will not find self-employment or low-productivity employment in agriculture, especially if opportunities for employment wane in other economic sectors. Present technologies, scale of production, and marketing arrangements may change in agriculture if future economic activity slows and energy sources decline.

9. Unemployment problems have existed in the recent past for young workers 16-19 years old, black and other nonwhite races, and young veterans 20-24 years old. Unemployment rates have also been somewhat above average for blue-collar workers of all kinds.

10. Levels of educational attainment are expected to increase among US workers. There will be an oversupply of college-educated workers during 1980-85, although the gap is not likely to be as high as the 700,000 figure projected by the Bureau of Labor Statistics. This will create a problem for the graduates and a bigger problem for those with whom they are competing for employment.

11. The labor force educational attainment is rising as older, relatively less-educated workers retire and the relatively better-educated young people replace them or are added into new positions.

Society

There are many important variables that impact on education and the educational attainment levels of people. We have already seen, for example, that demographic trends arising from births affect the school-age populations that correspond to various education levels. For elementary and secondary levels, the impact of changing birth patterns is straightforward. There is close to 100 percent attendance by age groups. In higher education, where aggregate individual decisions on participation must be considered, demographic data can only supply information on base populations from which the institutions draw their students. Some of the social and economic forces and policies that influence people to attend higher educational institutions are important and should be explored, if only briefly. Income levels, tuition costs, and student aid have clear and direct influence on enrollment.

Education has almost always been seen, and billed itself, as an avenue for upward mobility. As such, education will probably continue to hold promise to blacks and other nonwhites and to women as they seek greater equality of opportunity with whites and men respectively. As jobs become harder to find at all levels those with less education may also look to education as a method of avoiding unemployment. In particular as jobs tighten up for college graduates, the lack of employment opportunities and general job dissatisfaction may influence young people to seek to improve their employable skills through vocational training at the secondary and postsecondary levels.

There is also a certain amount of cultural consumption in education—that is, education is generally considered to be a good thing in and of itself. Aside from potential benefits like financial success or increased social status that might accrue to individuals with higher education, unadorned knowledge is considered to be a positive asset. Lack of alternative opportunities is also a tendency, albeit a rather negative one, that may influence larger numbers of people to seek further education. With high unemployment among the young, many of them could be expected to continue their education because of the lack of employment opportunities. Another influence which goes along with this is continuation of the lockstep mentality built into many young people today: primary school, high school, college, and graduate school follow in logical progression, until a person has spent twenty-five years or so of his or her life in school.

Finally, however, there is a psychosociological reason that may keep the college-educated supply high. Increased education breeds a mental expectation. A person has not become pegged at a given job or status level. A feeling of open-ended options prevails, and the realities of searching for jobs and making one's way seem somehow less real when a person is occupied in the school environment.

On the other hand, there are tendencies in society that may signal a movement away from increased participation in education. Certainly demographic factors forecast a considerable slowing or stabilization to the growth of higher education. The base population of young people will fall in the 1980s and the percentage of those 20-24 years of age receiving a high-school diploma is approaching 90 percent and slowing considerably. Unless colleges actively recruit and stimulate the attendance of age groups that have not traditionally participated in higher education, enrollments seem bound to alter drastically from the rapid expansion of the 1960s and early 1970s. In addition, increased numbers of young people may find it attractive to spend time in travel or gaining other valuable experience in work and leisure before continuing formal schooling.

It is also entirely possible that the continued expansion of higher education may not happen as expected in the traditional postsecondary institutions, but rather in an expansion of continuing education among adults. This makes sense from the point of view of colleges themselves. Colleges could conceivably enter the eighties with a declining population base and no further increases in the participation rates of the young. To the extent that they are already overextended financially, it may suggest that colleges should expand the age pool from which students are chosen. Continuing education provides substantial attraction to most adults in the US and initiatives by colleges to expand offerings in recurrent education would seem to have advantages for adults and colleges alike. This may bring a move closer to the open-entry/exit arrangements advocated by educators who envision a lifelong educational opportunity for all citizens.

Needs Deducible from Demographic, Economic, and Social-Background Projections

The Client Groups

This section attempts to deduce future needs from the demographic, economic, and social background traced out in the previous section. Education and employment requirements derive from the needs of two broad client groups, employees and employers. The characteristics of the former group have already been described in the analysis of the labor force in the previous section. However, little attention has been directed thus far to what employers need and want. Barring some rather radical changes, they can be expected to respond to the increased education of the work force the same as they have in the past. In the past, with better-educated applicants available, employers have raised educational requirements for entry jobs. In the past, the raising of entry-level educational requirements has had a variety of causes: increased complexity in the job as the technology develops; changes in the content of jobs without changes in occupational rubrics; perceived contributions of schooling apart from specific vocational training, i.e., socialization and acculturation that derive from general education. The raising of standards also reflects the function of the school as a selection process which screens out some job candidates with personal or social traits that employers view as undesirable. Also there is prestige derived from hiring people with high formal academic qualifications, when they are available in the labor market at little or no extra cost to the employer. Credentialism is a loose term to describe hiring based on education attainment seemingly in excess of that required to perform the job. It does affect employer hiring decisions, whatever its exact nature is.

With a slowing of growth in job openings requiring advanced education, and with a steady output from higher education and consequent large supply of highly educated workers, employers may hire increasing numbers of workers who are seemingly educated beyond the job requirement. This may reflect credentialism, or prestige or education as a selection modality, or some employer's notion of merit in education itself, or superior skill in job-seeking behavior by educated candidates. Whatever the cause, it is likely to result in the hiring of educated workers and displacement of workers with less formal education. Evidence on the effects of a mismatch between education and job level is mixed, but increased dissatisfaction is suggested for workers in some job situations.[25] In the past, at least in periods of high growth, the problem has been small because numbers affected have been small. If the magnitude of the problem increases markedly in future years, it is impossible to predict the consequences. With many faring the same, tensions may decrease; or, with a vast increase of workers even moderately dissatisfied, the problem may become serious for employers. An oversupply of educated workers, if accompanied by increased demands from workers dissatisfied by their jobs, may also increase the willingness of employers to adopt a positive response toward open-entry, open-exit education that would allow employees time off for continued education.

The Wants of the Client Groups

The wants of employer and employee groups are not expected to change much over the next fifteen years. There is no reason to expect employees to shift from present desires for steady employment, income, marriage, meaningfulness in job, security, and participation in activities that add a fullness to one's life.

Employers will continue to seek production, steadiness, and an acceptable employee demeanor. In attempting to lower per unit production costs employers have in the past defined job responsibilities more narrowly. However, there is a point where increased narrowing of jobs seems to lead to job dissatisfaction, worker absenteeism, and other worker characteristics that actually increase production costs. Thus, while employees may want more broadly defined jobs with greater responsibility and requiring more training, employers generally want more narrowly defined jobs requiring less training in an effort to cut production costs.[26] The resolution of these wants to the mutual satisfaction of both client groups will have to involve work redesign, job restructuring, and innovative work-related education programs.

The Need of the Client Groups

The need of the client groups actually comes to the heart of the future direction that work-related education programs must take. Table 2-20 attempts to analyze the needs of various employee groups that will arise because of the projected demographic, economic, and social factors that are likely to change over the next fifteen years. Table 2-20 indicates decreased pressures on providing entry-level training to the young. This may mean less need for work-related education programs designed to alleviate the youth unemployment situation. Along with this will come increased attention to the problems of older

Table 2-20
Future U.S. Education and Training Needs Arising from Demographic, Economic, and Social Projections

EMPLOYMENT STATUS	EMPLOYMENT CHARACTERISTICS	CHARACTERISTICS FROM DEMOGRAPHIC AND ECONOMIC PROJECTIONS	FUTURE EDUCATIONAL TRAINING NEEDS AND IMPLICATIONS FROM PROJECTIONS
Not in labor force	Home responsibilities	Increased tendency to return to work, even with small children	Somewhat unknown needs: guidance, placement, skill training, work incentives such as day-care: all increasing needs
	Students In college or college bound	Stabilizing in numbers; increased minority and female participation	Career exploration, career information, employment creation
	Non-college bound	Declining youth population; increasing non-college emphasis for education	Marketable job skills; guidance, counseling, placement
	Not employed, think they can't find work	—	Preemployment services; skill training for entry level jobs
Labor force	General labor force	Changing age patterns: 16-19 years: decreasing numbers	Entry level job training: less demographic pressure on needs of the young
		25-34 years: increasing numbers	Job upgrading, job redefinition and enrichment: increasing need
		55 and older: increasing slightly in numbers, retiring earlier, relatively low education levels	Self-employment, skill retraining for reemployment: increasing need

Unemployed	Seeking work	Changing sex patterns: Women: increased participation, earlier retirement, increased educational attainment	Training and retraining for occupational diversification
		Men: decreased participation, earlier retirement, increased educational attainment	Decreased pressure on needs of men in general relative to women
		Changing racial patterns Negro and other races: increase relative percentage of population; expected continued high unemployment	Entry level training or retraining; preemployment services for unemployed; job creation
		Continued structural differences by race and occupations and industries: high for Negroes, low for white collar, low for government, etc.	Entry level training, preemployment services
Underemployed	Low skills	Increasing in numbers, especially among the college educated	Skill upgrading
	Too highly educated		Needs for job upgrading, job creation, or skill retraining: need increasing
Employed	Low skills	——	Skill upgrading
	Job dissatisfaction	——	Job enrichment, unexplored
	Employable skills and job satisfaction	——	Minor needs

established workers who need job enrichment, job upgrading, and provision for continuing education. Women are expected to experience occupational shifts toward managerial and administrative jobs. Highly educated women will find additional employment in manufacturing and trade, and no longer be limited to opportunities in the services. They may require preemployment services in guidance and placement, along with a certain amount of job retraining or upgrading. Minority groups will still need entry-level training, skill improvement and upgrading, and pre-employment services.

An assured level of productivity and employee stability may be necessary before employers will participate willingly in work-related education programs. For example, cooperative and work/study programs, while establishing good community relations, often have high absenteeism, and require individual counseling, transportation, and health care, only to yield decreased productivity as the student begins the training process. Employers often demand greater flexibility in school scheduling and staffing policies and updated school curric-ulum and teaching materials to make the training more relevant to employer objectives. In addition, job enrichment and enlargement programs have often been described as successful by employers when viewed from the perspective of benefits that accrue to employers as well as employees, yet most remain both small in scale and poorly evaluated.[27]

Resources for Responding to Needs

Previous sections have described the needs of employee or potential employee groups as they develop over the next fifteen years in response to demographic, economic, and social changes. This projection serves for charting the direction of changing needs. However, it is worthwhile to look at present needs and the extent to which these needs are being met, because the present response to present needs must form the base upon which future response to changing needs is built. By almost any standard of provision the present response is inadequate. This section briefly explores the present response to the work-related education needs of two groups: (1) the unemployed, underemployed, and those not in the labor force who would like to work; and (2) secondary-level students.

Data detailing the characteristics of trainees enrolled in selected training programs administered by the Department of Labor during fiscal year 1973 clearly indicate that the programs are being directed at groups most seriously in need.[28] Over 44 percent of enrollees were women, nearly equal to their representation on the rolls of the unemployed. Blacks represented some 40 percent of all enrollees, a figure nearly double their proportion of unemployed workers. Young people accounted for 60 percent of total enrollments, well in excess of their 38 percent share of unemployment. And workers forty-five years and older represented some 52 percent of enrollees in Operation Mainstream. In addition the unemployed, underemployed, and those not in the labor force represented the majority in all programs that reported such enrollee characteristics.

While the programs are generally addressing the right people, the total numbers involved are extremely small when compared to the number of people in need. Table 2-21 shows Department of Labor work and training programs by the prior employment characteristics of the trainees. While a good portion of the data is missing (the table shows only 468,500 of the 1,538,000 trainees in 1973), indications are clear that these programs enroll only a small portion of those who could potentially benefit. Obviously not all those who are unemployed, for example, desire or need such programs, and it is unrealistic to assume that there are 4.3 million unemployed in need of work and training programs. However, Table 2-21 shows that only some 436,400 trainees were unemployed prior to receiving training in the 1973 Department of Labor programs that reported prior employment characteristics of trainees. Of the approximately 984,000 trainees for which data were not available, many were undoubtedly unemployed prior to enrollment. The number of unemployed persons served is still only a fraction of the number unemployed. Also, the number of people out of the labor force and not enrolled in these programs is very small compared to the number of persons not in the labor force who report that they would like work.

At the state level the inadequacies in size of these programs is also evident. Taking Operation Mainstream as an example, one finds that enrollment opportunities in the state of Massachusetts total only 300.[29] This program is the only Department of Labor program with the majority of the enrollees older than forty-five, and yet the response is minimal. The 1970 Census for the state of Massachusetts shows a total of 1,848,000 people forty-five years of age or older.[30]

Department of Labor programs appear to be meeting only a small percentage of the potential need for work-related education among the unemployed, underemployed, and those not in the labor force. Program responses described in previous sections could be considered only a very inadequate response to satisfying present unmet needs. The large increases in the age groups 25-44 represents an example of changing patterns outlined in previous sections. Increased efforts in job upgrading and enrichment will be required for this group. The objective must compete with the still largely unmet needs of those people who are unemployed or of those who are not in the work force but would like to be employed. With limited resources the problem will demand careful ordering of priority among groups needing assistance.

The enrollments in vocational education make it appear that programs are serving a substantial percentage of secondary level students (see Table 2-22). The 7,232,000 secondary students enrolled in federally aided vocational-technical education programs in 1972 represents 51 percent of all students in regular and

Table 2-21
Total First-Time Enrollments in Department of Labor Administered Work and Training Programs by Prior Employment Characteristic of Enrollees, Fiscal Year 1973, and Potential Target Population for Such Programs in 1973
(in thousands)

PROGRAM	TOTAL FIRST-TIME ENROLLMENTS	TOTAL–FIRST TIME ENROLLMENTS BY PRIOR EMPLOYMENT STATUS OF ENROLLEES				TOTALS
		Not in labor force, want job now	Unemployed	Underemployed	Other	
MDTA Institutional training[1]	119.6	13.6	78.2	16.3	11.5	119.6
JOP-OJT	147.5	—	—	—	—	—
Neighborhood Youth Corps In-school[2]	553.7	—	—	—	—	—
Out-of-school	74.7	9.1	62.6	2.2	0.7	74.6
Operation Mainstream	37.5	2.3	32.0	2.7	0.6	37.6
Public Service Careers	24.6	—	—	—	—	—
Concentrated Employment Program	68.8	0.8	64.9	2.4	0.7	68.8
JOBS (federally funded)	51.5	—	—	—	—	—
Work Incentive Program	238.5	—	—	—	—	—
Job Corps	43.4	—	—	—	—	—
Public Employment Program	177.9	—	162.2	15.7	—	177.9
Totals	1537.7	25.8	399.9	39.3	13.5	478.5
Potential target population		4,460	4,304	2,311[3]	—	11,075

[1] Administered jointly with HEW [2] Includes summer programs [3] Persons on part-time for economic reasons: nonagricultural

SOURCE: Adapted from data in U.S. Department of Labor, 1974 **Manpower Report of the President**, pp. 263, 271, 285, 358, 362, and 367.

Table 2-22
Enrollments in Federally Aided Vocational-Technical Education, by Type of Program, Fiscal Year 1972

(In thousands)

Program Type	Total	Enrollments			Percent Distribution
		Secondary	Post-secondary	Adult	
Agriculture	896	603	35	258	7.7
Distribution	640	263	103	275	5.5
Health	337	59	177	100	2.9
Home economics, gainful	280	162	38	80	2.4
Consumer and home-making	3,166	2,469	31	666	27.3
Office	2,352	1,508	360	484	20.3
Technical	337	39	189	109	2.9
Trades and industry	2,398	952	357	1,089	20.7
Special[a]	1,305	1,223	46	36	11.2
Totals	11,602	7,232	1,304	3,066	100.0

[a]Includes enrollments in exemplary, prevocational, prepostsecondary, and remedial programs.
Source: U.S. Department of Labor, *1974 Manpower Report of the President*, p. 372.

other public secondary schools in that year.[31] However, when these programs are broken down into programs involving actual work experience, the coverage appears far different. In the state of Massachusetts, total public secondary enrollments during 1972 were 356,600, and by 1978 this figure is expected to reach 403,380.[32] While those enrolled in gainful vocational programs during 1972 totaled 30 percent of all public secondary students, the percentage involved in actual work experience (work/study or cooperative education) amounted to 0.7 percent of those in secondary school.[33] By 1978 this is expected to have grown to 0.9 percent of those in secondary school. Thus, a very small number of students will be experiencing work in a nonschool setting.

In general, current work-related education programs do not meet the needs of large numbers of people, either in providing assistance to the unemployed and underemployed or in providing actual work experience to secondary students. With large unmet present needs and a slowing economy in the eighties, it will take a substantially increased emphasis on human resource investment to address more fully the present needs and the changing needs of the future.

3 Work and Education

Introduction

By convention, formal or academic schooling is contrasted with work. In academic schooling, teacher/pupil/book/classroom are joined, and cognitive learning is the major outcome; in work, the object is the production of goods and services, although learning may be a by-product. In reality the distinctions between work and schooling are not that clear; and across the years and cultures of man, education and work have been bound together in form, substance, and purpose. Schooling is one form of work, for in scholarship knowledge is produced, and through instruction services are provided; but education is only one of the many important human products and services. Work may also educate, inasmuch as in performance of the activity, behavior may be modified to improve performance in subsequent rounds; thus, learning takes place. Yet much of the general knowledge vital to a culture is not best transmitted through work.

Formal schooling is a limited form of productive activity and productive work is a limited form of educational activity, but the differences are significant enough so that the activities are separated and specialized. Between the two there are many blends and shadings, as Figure 4-1 (p. 86) indicates. The knowledge yielded in formal schooling is more general, and has referrents in a wider domain of time and place, than the more specific knowledge gained in work. Professional education is nearer to general academic education in this respect, vocational education further along on the dimension of specificity, and apprenticeship and on-job training very close to productive work itself. The same kind of range characterizes education for the performance of societal roles, which include, but are not limited to, work roles. General education is designed as a preparation for multiple roles; professional and vocational education narrow toward preparing for single or more specific role requirements, and work-based training is even more specific, being limited to the role of producer in one work situation. Both formal schooling and work impart and improve skills, with schooling designed to develop skills that enhance cognitive learning; whereas work sometimes, but by no means always, provides practice for improvement of skills.

Although the contrast is in part a stereotype, a shading from cognitive learning to development of skills runs from general to professional to technical to vocational education, and on to apprenticeship training and work itself. At

63

least this is so of some fields of training and work. The shading from abstract to concrete knowledge runs from general education through vocational training to the work situation; as does immediacy or directness with which the acquired knowledge, skills, and attitudes can be applied. Academic education is often remote in time and place from job performance, but all manner of blends of work and schooling attempt to moderate this separation through experiences that range from simulation of the reality of production in vocational schooling to direct production in on-job training.

Professional and vocational education programs are designed, though not exclusively, to prepare for subsequent entry to work, whereas combinations of on-job experience and training are more often to aid workers in adapting to performance demands within the context of work. In Figure 4-1 general and vocational education are in a segment called "preparation," whereas on-job and apprenticeship training are in a segment called "adaptation," but between the two are a variety of combinations of education and work experience designed to improve human performance in one limited but important outcome—production. These blends of work and education have developed over the years in a wide variety of settings in the United States and other countries.

Programs to prepare people to find, enter, and maintain employment, to adapt to changing work requirements, and to improve job and career opportunities have evolved slowly and at an uneven pace over the past three centuries in the United States. For the first two centuries men learned their jobs by performing the work and emulating the master. This was true even for high offices and demanding professions. Medicine and the law were largely learned by working at the profession. For the higher offices, such education as there was was suited mainly for clergymen and classical scholars. For the lesser arts and trades, if there was any general educational foundation it provided minimal literacy, not so much to prepare for job performance, but to mold character and perfect moral and spiritual performance. The trade was learned through long indenture and apprenticeship, and this pattern persisted until a century ago. Vocational education, formal schooling explicitly designed to prepare man for work, has had only a hundred years of history in the United States.

Apprenticeship

Apprenticeship is the oldest mode of preparing men for work, and the practice has threaded its way through work-related education and training programs down to the present time. Programs that developed out of the Manpower Development and Training Act of 1962 and the Economic Opportunity Act of 1964 and that compendium of most recent legislation governing employment and training, the Comprehensive Employment and Training Act of 1973, still incorporate the essential feature of apprenticeship, the training of workers on the job and directly in the production process itself. These are precisely the programs that are hailed as most innovative, which demonstrates one curious feature of work-related education in the United States and in other countries: program approaches tend to appear and disappear over time and be hailed as new when they come back into prominence. This is also the case with work-based education in China. In the United States, in the last quarter of the nineteenth century, apprenticeship, which had been the pattern for two hundred years, was looked upon as the old-fashioned way; and the first vocational schools were coming in as the new way to train men for work.

A variety of circumstances account for the rise of industrial and trade-school education in the U.S., and the end of sole reliance on apprenticeship training. The pace of industrialization was quickening and the demand for bench and machine workers in industry was drawing migrant workers in from rural regions of the United States and Europe. Immigrant workers appeared in large numbers and were not judged fit by general education and experience to cope with mechanization and the growing sophistication of the technology of the time. Apprenticeship was too long and slow, and depended for success on stable work forces bound by family ties and cultural homogeneity. In the manufacturing process itself work was being rationalized and fragmented into bits and pieces that were not readily learned in a master-apprentice relationship. Also, the unions were gaining strength, and the industrialists sought to break the hold of trades and guilds over the training and certification of workers.

The unions at first resisted the development of industrial training schools and trade schools, but by 1910 the American Federation of Labor through its Committee of Industrial Education was criticizing apprenticeship as slow, wasteful, and inefficient, and attempted to shape the pattern of vocational training that had been developing in the schools. The Committee on Industrial Education of the AFL recommended continuation schools to improve the skills of young employed workers, supplemental trade schools, and publicly run trade schools that would offer a mix of general education and shop training. So that they might not lose control over the new form of vocational education the unions strongly recommended that the schools be guided by advisory boards with union and management represented. Again this has been a recurrent theme in the history of the development of work-related education. Down to the present time critics of vocational education have pressed for more effective use of union and management representatives to keep vocational education programs relevant to the work world and responsive to the labor market.

Though the movement was away from apprenticeship in the early years of this century, on-the-job training continued as a recurrent though muted theme of vocational education; and in many of the more stable and traditional shops of the Northeast, apprenticeship programs in the old style have survived until recent times. The Smith Hughes Act of 1917, the first major legislation and the foundation of school-based vocational education, provided that vocational agricultural programs must offer six months of actual and supervised farming experience. For trade and industrial programs the requirement was only that about half the training hours be spent in school shops. During periods of slow growth in industrial employment in the twenties there was recurrent support for on-job training. A major motive may have been to reduce public expenditures during times when revenues dipped with earnings and income. The underlying logic was of course faulty, inasmuch as declining employment opportunities decreased the possibilities of work sites for training and production combined. The more sensible policy would seem to have been to hold young people off the labor market as long as possible in formal schools, vocational or otherwise. In reality this is what happened.

Between World War I and II there was intermittent favor for apprenticeship. The Advisory Committee on Education issued a host of conclusions and recommendations in 1938, stressing the centrality of general education but pointing out the weaknesses of school-based vocational education. The Committee recommended an increase in apprenticeship programs. In the Depression years and subsequently, when the costs of vocational education in schools weighed heavily, apprenticeship was suggested as a way to shift the burden onto private industries and off the public fisc. In both world wars, where there was a sudden spurt in demand for skilled workers, because the old form of lengthy and formal apprenticeship could not serve, the on-job-training feature was incorporated into accelerated and segmented training courses. After World War II, when there was a vast retraining of war workers and veterans in prospect, Secretary of Labor Perkins stated: "It has been demonstrated that for many types of jobs, apprenticeship and other forms of training within industry give better results and can be carried on at less expense than vocational education in the schools."[1] The major legislation that followed this testimony, the George Barden Act (1946), did not redirect vocational education toward apprenticeship training, however. Though apprenticeship training was from time to time supported for reasons of nostalgia, economy, or its presumed effectiveness in training for employment, and though private industries continued to support apprentice programs, public support in the period from the Smith Hughes Act to the Vocational Education Act amendments of 1968 went primarily to school-based vocational education.

Over the years, school-based vocational education was criticized as costly, outmoded, remote from production reality, and ineffective and inadequate, but it prevailed and still flourishes. Although the costs of vocational schooling were obvious, the presumed benefits of vocational school training versus apprentice training were not systematically assessed. A more fundamental problem was that no assessment was ever made of how willing private industry was to remove the burden of vocational training from the public fisc, except in those cases where the specific needs of an industry were directly served by such training. The issues of cost-effectiveness and benefit-costs of vocational schooling versus on-job training seem to be still unanalyzed and unresolved, and may be unresolvable in the general case. The issue may yield a pseudoquestion, like the age-old query, "What is the ideal teacher-pupil ratio in primary schools?" for which there is no general answer.

School-Based Vocational Education

School-based vocational education has appeared under varying forms, beginning in the last quarter of the nineteenth century. One pattern was full-time day attendance for youth preparing to enter mechanical fields in industry. An early example was the mechanic arts program at Massachusetts Institute of Technology, based on the "Russian Plan" developed by Della Vos.[2] In outline, the approach simulated the production situation. By abstracting and systematizing the process, the materials and steps were arranged so as to emphasize teaching and learning rather than production. A second approach was embodied in the New York Trades School, where the elements of the construction trades were taught. Designed more narrowly to prepare workers for the trades, and incidentally to shake off union control of apprenticeship training, the trade-school model was less favored by liberals and educators who criticized it as narrow and rigid, classbound, and ultimately less productive of general learning.

A third strand running down through school-based vocational education came out of the Manual Training School at Washington University, which emphasized manual-skill development as a necessary part of general education. Further development in mechanic arts programs also led to the view that learning mechanical principles in applied situations fostered general intellectual growth. These notions, developing through time, brought the inclusion of manual training and industrial arts into programs of general education.

To remove the isolation and class bias of trade and vocational schools, the comprehensive school, offering both vocational and general programs, was periodically favored, although this was not a movement that would gain force for another fifty years. The participation of universities and quality technical and scientific institutes in the founding of manual training and mechanic arts programs provided prestigious support to vocational education in the United States. By 1910 full-time day vocational education was an established part of North American education, backed by powerful supporters. The American Federation of Labor representing the unions, the National Association of Manufacturers representing industry and the National Education Association were advocating establishment of full-time day vocational and part-time continuation schools for employed youth, and night schools for adult workers.

To the urban industrial interests supporting vocational education were added rural and agricultural forces then attempting to advance agricultural extension and training through the Smith Lever Act. Again, though the main support burden was borne by agrarian leadership groups such as the Grange, higher education offered collateral support coming from the agricultural and A&M colleges. The result was the Smith Hughes Act, which in 1917 moved the federal government behind vocational schooling. Patterns established under this legislation lasted down to present times, for good or ill. The pattern of federal-state matching support gave vocational education a separate and independent status that has bothered general educators to this day. Vocational schools have proven difficult to bring under local control as part of general education, and resistant to more flexible manpower development and training initiatives of recent times. The separation was criticized by the President's Advisory Committee on Education and again by Rogers,[3] and the sad effect for manpower development has been noted by Ruttenberg.[4] Cases collected for training school administrators at Harvard Graduate School of Education in the mid-fifties detail jurisdictional battles between local superintendents and directors of vocational schools.[5] The pattern of half-shop and half-general education has also lasted until the Vocational Education acts and amendments of 1963 and 1968.

The agrarian support did not come without price, and home economics and vocational agricultural programs accounted for major shares in the enrollments in the years between the wars, despite declining agricultural employment possibilities after World War I. As late as 1965, 16 percent of the enrollments in federally aided vocational schools were in agriculture and 38 percent in consumer and homemaking courses. Some home economics programs were adapted to food industry jobs.

Over the years between the world wars the George Reed, George Ellsey, and George Dean acts added bits and pieces to the basic Smith Hughes Act. Distributive education was added to the basic agriculture, home economics, and trade education programs. As the demand for agricultural employment steadily declined with the shift in economic activity and the continuing rise in agricultural productivity, the enrollments in agricultural programs became more disproportionate to demand. Full-time enrollment in trades and industry programs did not match corresponding employment in these sectors. In 1926 only 10 percent of the enrollment in trades and industry programs were full-time day students. As the Depression settled in during the early thirties, enrollments in vocational programs increased, simply because there were no jobs to be found; but because support stayed steady or was cut, the quality and coverage of the programs worsened.

The two problems, unresponsiveness to employment demand and low support for relatively high cost programs, were to plague vocational education up through World War II. The demand for skilled workers generated by the war boom was met by other training arrangements, and this was noted in the section on apprenticeship and on-job training. War manpower mobilization and training of workers to weather the Great Depression were covered by legislation and organizations outside the vocational establishment (a fact to be noted in a later section). Programs developed under the Federal Emergency Relief Administration (FERA), the Works Progress Administration (WPA), the Civilian Conservation Corps (CCC) and National Youth Administration (NYA) proved much better models for later manpower development, employment, and training programs under MDTA and OEO. The conventional vocational school programs evolving out of Smith Hughes and the various bills sponsored under the name of Senator George were not the appropriate models for the more innovative programs of the sixties, where the objective was to reach deprived groups needing special kinds of training, work experience, and employment-support services that are described in later chapters. It would also seem that the Depression-spawned programs may be much better models for future programs that attempt to respond to very heavy unemployment, where the problem is not so much to train for standardized and existing jobs as to create employment and new jobs.

Constructive criticism and reform proposals for vocational education were offered over the years, the previous quote by Frances Perkins (p. 66) being an example. In the discussions and hearings preceding the George Barden Act (1946),[6] a broadening of the offerings to include training for office and public service occupations was extensively discussed, as was the need to support vocational guidance in order to improve the fit between vocational education and work. The general notion that vocational programs should be at least in part shaped by labor force demand was also advanced, but the bill, much of it never funded and implemented, was pretty much the same mixture as before.

In the fifties vocational education did not flourish, but some new program fields were added. The impetus furnished by Sputnik, resulting in the National Defense Education Act, did bring one new and important emphasis, the shift of attention to technical training at the postsecondary level. Over the next two decades many of the newer programs in the technical fields would shift from secondary level to postsecondary technical schools and junior colleges. With a vast increase in junior-college development in the offing, vocational programs at the technical or subprofessional level would expand to provide engineering associates, laboratory technicians, and new specialists in the public service fields. Postsecondary institutions, under local and state government, and private auspices, with state and federal support, proved more flexible and responsive to new demands for technically trained manpower. Postsecondary institutions were thought to provide more adequate terminal training in the technical fields.[7] The postsecondary schools were also more flexible in providing continuing access to higher education, and hence were freer of charges of isolation and rigidity that were leveled at secondary-level vocational schools.

The criticisms of vocational education, which had been mounting over the years from Smith Hughes through George Reed and George Barden, were reviewed in the early sixties by the Panel of Consultants on Vocational Education (Willis Committee). One result was the Vocational Education Act of 1963, originally part of an omnibus education bill. New program categories, especially in office occupations and distributive education for retail trade employment, were strengthened and shaped to the demand for employment that had been growing in these fields. Higher-level technical programs, below college level and in new fields outside defense related industry, were strengthened. Rigidities in trade training, which prescribed 50 percent shop work, and in vocational agriculture, which required farm practice, were loosened. Rigidities in categorical allocations were relaxed. Home economics was directed more toward employment. The most important changes, however, were not limited to minor programmatic modifications, but sought fundamental changes:

1. Groups with special needs were singled out for special training, job support, and assistance. This brought vocational education more in line with initiatives that were being developed from MDTA and OEO legislation. Design of service for deprived groups represents a program priority that has continued to the present time.

2. Support was provided for research and development efforts aimed at design and trial of innovative and exemplary programs for work-related education.

3. The new legislation also recognized the importance of economic planning, to develop and expand vocational education programs in accord with economic development and manpower needs. The relationship between vocational schools and the Employment Service, which would provide job market information, was strengthened.

4. Funds for extended supportive services in counseling and guidance and placement were provided, especially to assist disadvantaged groups experiencing difficulties in gaining employment.

5. There was more stress on flexible programs to train adults and youths for employment. The notion was that the program should be shaped to the job demand and client availability and need, rather than the reverse. Though, as the next section will indicate, there had from the earliest times been programs of part-time and continuation study for young people, the new arrangements were to be even more flexible, in an attempt to reach out to deprived groups with work and learning problems engendered by poverty.

Although the Vocational Education Act of 1963 had many new and important features, little of it was put into practice, and for the next few years most of the innovative features were exemplified primarily in programs carried out by OEO and MDTA. For this reason, the Advisory Panel, after monitoring the programs, reported lack of progress, especially in the newer initiatives, and voiced criticisms that led to the amendments of 1968. The amendments of 1968 attempted to strengthen the implementation of the Vocational Education Act of 1963. Some of the newer features of the old act, languishing unimplemented, were supported. The concept of the responsibility of vocational education was broadened to include development of employable skills through prevocational training and counseling support, provision of remedial general education which would enhance employability, and assistance in job-placement and job-supporting services. These latter initiatives were more often realized through the OEO and MDTA programs than through conventional vocational education, but at least the need had been identified in the legislation and the responsibility accepted by vocational educators.

Developments in formal school-based vocational education, traced from the beginnings of manual training and mechanics arts schools in the late nineteenth century down to the newer initiatives of the 1960s, may have suggested that the main development was through full-time day-school attendance. This was not the case, for through the years part-time study for employed and unemployed workers was always a common pattern. In some periods part-time study was the prevalent pattern, and enrollments of part-time students were higher than full-time in vocational programs.

Part-time, Continuing, and Adult
Education for Employment

The blending of periods of work and schooling has been a recurrent pattern from the earliest years in the United States, when intermittent schooling was put into the unrelieved work rounds of children and adults, through Sunday schools and night schools. In agrarian settings schooling in literacy and morals was fitted around the crop seasons, the work week, and the work day. It may seem that in two centuries in the United States the practice has circled back, although by no means completely. Current career-education programs, incorporating work/study and cooperative education, appear to represent an attempt to introduce work and production experience into formal and academic school programs.

Even when apprenticeship training was in decline and vocational schooling on the rise, at the beginning of the century, there were authoritative voices recommending more effective blends of work training and academic schooling. The Douglass Commission report on industrial and technical education (Massachusetts, 1906) criticized schooling for being overly literary and irrelevant for preparing young people for work.[8] Manual training was viewed as empty and ritualistic. The Commission recommended that vocational training for industry and agriculture be incorporated into regular school programs at the earliest grade levels. Among other influential recommendations was the proposal that part-time day schooling be offered for young workers (ages 14 to 18) who had left full-time academic study to earn their livelihoods. In 1910 the American Federation of Labor, then moving into vocational education and away from advocacy of apprenticeship training, recommended that publicly supported continuation schools be established for young workers, and that union-aided supplementary trade programs be offered for adults.[9] The Smith Hughes Act (1917) provided for both part-time schools for employed youth fourteen years and older and evening schools for adult workers.

In the years following Smith Hughes, as periodic recessions reduced industrial manpower demands, part-time attendance in industrial and trade training programs was more common than full-time vocational education. This tendency was encouraged by the decline in revenues available for more costly vocational-training programs in intermittent depressed times after World War I. In 1926 over 90 percent of the vocational enrollments in the trade and industrial fields were part-time. Young workers in continuation schools were required to attend four to six hours weekly, and some pre-employment courses were developed and made available on a part-time basis. In the Great Depression full-time enrollments increased in vocational programs, not by design or conscious rejection of the part-time programs. but mainly because outside jobs were not available, especially for young workers.

In recent years, part-time vocational training has been offered under a variety of legislative headings and through many different program arrangements. Special programs for deprived and handicapped groups came out of the Vocational Education Act of 1963 and the amendments of 1968. Children with handicaps preventing full-time attendance, institutionalized or partially institutionalized youngsters, and socially and economically deprived clients who could not or would not attend full-time programs were served in specially adapted part-time and night-school programs. The Neighborhood Youth Corps provided opportunities for supplemental work experience, training, and earning to youngsters in and out of school.

The Job Corps set up vocational training centers, as well as making arrangements for part-time vocational and general education. Comprehensive manpower-development programs contracted with centers and vocational schools for supplementary vocational training, as well as remedial general education, prevocational orientation, and job-support counseling. Adult workers were given entitlement to night trade training to upgrade job skills. Mixes of apprenticeship, or on-job training, and part-time vocational and general education were developed. During periods of war mobilization the facilities of vocational schools were used for part-time training to supplement or extend on-job training. However, though part-time and continuation programs have been a central part of vocational training along with full-time attendance, in periods when there was a need to mobilize manpower either to win through a depression or a war, or to take on a burden of providing opportunity to large deprived groups, much of the main action has been based outside of conventional school settings.

Mobilization for Manpower Development

Neither apprenticeship, nor full-time vocational schooling, nor part-time night and continuation schooling has proven sufficient when the United States has been forced to mobilize and develop manpower on a large scale for some special situation. All three approaches have served part of the general mobilization purposes, but none has been sufficient. When the object of the mobilization has been war, with a demand for a rapid expansion of production and a limited supply of male workers in prime working age groups, apprenticeship programs and vocational schooling have not produced the numbers of trained workers in the limited time available to train them. In the wars, large numbers of women, workers outside the prime work-age groups, and minority groups left out of past work opportunities have had to be brought into the work force, trained, and rapidly assimilated. Workers in jobs that are peripheral to war production have to be shifted and retrained.

Executives, chafing at what they view as rigidity and low responsiveness in the vocational schools and formal apprenticeship programs, develop new and accelerated forms of training close to the work site. This may seem to suggest that vocational schooling has been too rigid or sluggish to respond, although usually everyone is too busy or preoccupied to make this charge overtly. Vocational educators point out that resources have not been made available for innovative approaches on a large scale in normal times, but when emergency situations have arisen and funding has been made available, the vocational education establishment has provided the base for expanded programs. In World War I mobilization was slower and more partial, both in industrial and military manpower; but in World War II, in a five-year period, more than $300 million was allocated to equipping and supporting vocational training programs, and the total number of participants was approximately 7.5-million.[10] Trade, industrial, and technical training school programs were expanded out of normal patterns. When supplemented by extramural and on-site job-training extension, vocational schooling provided the base for expansion to meet the emergency. This was not so clearly the case when the country mobilized to confront other problems, and resources and support were contracting rather than expanding as in the war.

As the country confronted the Depression in the early thirties conventional apprenticeship and vocational school-based programs did not seem to offer the solution. Just as conventional monetary and fiscal policies and programs failed to respond to the magnitude of the general economic problem, so too did conventional manpower development, training, and employment programs fail to provide a sufficient response.

Jobs had to be created. The Federal Emergency Relief Agency (FERA), and later the Works Progress Administration (WPA), had to provide gainful employment for large numbers of untrained and unskilled workers. Unlike the Public Works programs (PWA), which essentially employed trained and experienced workers on larger and more ambitious construction projects, the FERA and WPA used untrained workers on a vast variety of small and scattered projects. In order that the projects not be pure make-work, with no worthwhile yield, there was a need to furnish training, however modest, and this the FERA and later the WPA did do.

FERA and WPA training programs also furnished employment for teachers and skilled workers; but the numbers involved, the background of the participants, and the scarce resources and urgent need for expansion produced training that did not meet quality standards of vocational educators. Criticisms such as one that appeared in the *American Vocational Association Journal* of 1935 reflected the resistance of the vocational education establishment to what was viewed as encroachment by incompetents:

Classes are thrown open to all comers regardless of their ability to profit by the instruction; the instructors are drawn from among persons on relief rolls; "shops" are inadequately equipped except in larger cities; insufficient and, frequently, no preliminary instructor training is given to inexperienced "teachers" ... and little or no supervision is given these teachers after they have organized their classes.[11]

All observations were perhaps true and fair within the limited perspective of the observers, but sadly missed the main point that special groups with special needs under special circumstances required approaches that were not conventional, even when the conventions seemed to be on the side of quality and standards. This situation was to be somewhat paralleled in the 1960s when a third need for mobilization arose, the so-called war on poverty and the major attempt to serve previously deprived and ignored client groups.

To the FERA and WPA training programs were added training under the National Youth Administration (NYA) and Civilian Conservation Corps (CCC). Criticism of these programs by vocational education groups was just as vehement and more or less on the same grounds. These programs also developed approaches that would later serve as models for Office of Economic Opportunity and Manpower Development and Training Act programs. Out of the WPA, CCC, and NYA programs come these important realizations:

1. It was feasible and in fact necessary to serve groups sunk far down in poverty and deprivation, and to provide services to large numbers in mass programs covering large areas.

2. It was recognized that these groups had special needs that could sometimes be best met with less formal academic instructional services provided outside normal school settings:

a. Vocational training in the CCC camps, though usually limited to less than ten hours a week, resembled later Job Corps camps and center programs, although the latter provided much more intensive skill training and immediate employment-support efforts.

b. Training in centers and in dispersed site projects under WPA and NYA provided models for MDTA and OEO developments of multiskill development centers and Neighborhood Youth Corps out-of-school programs.

c. Under the NYA some of the early forms that later led to cooperative and work/study education programs were developed. The notion of mixing academic schooling with paid work experience, though born of economic necessity in the Depression programs, became accepted for its educative value in later career-education programs.

d. Pre-employment training with work experience came out of the CCC and NYA programs.

e. Provision of part-time work experience and vestibule and protected jobs developed out of Depression experience, although the broadening of service to include handicapped and institutionalized groups was not generally accepted as a public charge that early. Other privately sponsored programs, e.g., the Salvation Army work and training shops, were developing these approaches in the earlier years.

3. Recognition of the importance of broadening mobilization programs to include training and job support for later employment came out of experience in the Depression year programs.

4. The notion of public service employment was clearly born of the Depression programs.

5. The need to provide supporting services, health, counseling, and remedial general education came out of the CCC, NYA, and other programs of the Depression years. CCC programs, for example, provided five or more hours a week of general and remedial education.

The Depression years were lean and hard ones, but from the challenge and the necessity of mobilizing public support programs to confront the difficulties came many policies and programs useful to guide later efforts in employment creation, work-related education and training, and employment support. The innovative range of education and employment-support programs that developed through the 1960s profited by experience born of the mobilization programs of the 1930s. One major approach was missing from the earlier programs, because of their essential limitations as a response to massive unemployment in private sector activity. Comprehensive manpower development programs that would cover the planning of employment and education and the development of jobs in private and public sector enterprises were not developed systematically until thirty years after the Depression, when the economy and employment were expanding.

Comprehensive Manpower Development:
Employment and Training

Comprehensive manpower development programs, which include job creation and job support and selection of training fields based on job market demand, have been mainly a development of the past decade. In the years after World War

II, although comprehensive manpower planning and development were becoming increasingly common in southern Europe and in the developing countries of the Third World, and though some of the originators of these programs were Americans (Parnes and Harbison),[1 2] activity in the United States was scattered, partial, and intermittent. Concern for one or another part of the comprehensive approach has flickered through the history of work-related education, long before the concentrated and comprehensive employment program trials of the 1960s resulted in the Comprehensive Employment and Training Act of 1973. The Douglass Commission Report (1906) stressed the need to make vocational training more responsive to the requirements of employment and industrial demand, and the American Federation of Labor Committee on Industrial Education (1910) stressed trade training in appropriate fields, and retraining for employed workers.

Discussions prior to the George Barden bill stressed the need to move out of fields where demand was falling and into office and public-service occupations where prospects were better. Training for re-entry of veterans and war-workers was to be in fields that responded to new and growing demands in the civilian economy. The legislation and programs that came out of the bill, however, did not fully realize the concerns raised in discussing it, and the old fields, voc-ag, trade-industrial (in limited fields), and home economics, pretty much dominated as before. The Willis Committee Report stressed response to demands of growing and emerging fields, especially at the technician level. The Vocational Education Act of 1963, which came out of the Willis Committee deliberations, stated that vocational-education programs should be calibrated to changing manpower requirements, and that there was to be a more effective linkage with job-finding and employment support services provided by the public employment service. There was an attempt to bring Department of Labor programs (employment service, labor market analysis, and later more comprehensive manpower development) closer to the vocational programs run under HEW auspices. The programs that came out of the legislation of 1963 did not actually do much in comprehensive manpower development terms, but the thought was there.

More direct movement toward comprehensive manpower development came out of the MDTA legislation and programs (1962) and the Economic Opportunity Act of 1964. For the deprived and handicapped groups, just beginning to be served under these legislative acts, it was apparent that far more than mere vocational schooling was necessary. The new clients had to be trained in jobs for which there was a clear, and, if possible, rising demand; for with so many other social and economic disadvantages, employment prospects for the deprived and handicapped were limited at best. These groups had to be helped to find a job and to hold a job, and this often meant providing a range of pre-employment services and experience, and continuing and follow-up support services during the early stages of employment. Once located in jobs, advancement and career development possibilities had to be opened up through retraining. Job redesign and enrichment were subsequent additions that will be dealt with later.

In some cases employment opportunities had to be created for the job aspirant, rather than merely providing training to adapt him to the job opportunity as it emerged. In public-sector employment, the policies and programs of the Depression years provided extensive experience that could be drawn on later. Activities under the Public Employment Program, Operation Mainstream, Neighborhood Youth Corps, Work Incentive Program, public service employment, and work/study opportunities were later programs to provide public employment that descended from earlier and similar efforts devised and tried in the Depression years. Perforce the Depression years offered little possibility for stimulating employment in private enterprises. This was to come later, in the economic-opportunity and manpower-development and training programs, through such programs as JOBS, in which public funds were used to encourage private sector employment creation. The job opportunity program, e.g., the programs under JOBS and the Construction Outreach Program, COP, also aimed to create work places for special groups.

Systematic and continuing attempts to plan training and employment-support programs according to labor market developments and manpower demands came under the Concentrated Employment Program and the Comprehensive Manpower Development programs, which flowed into the base for developing the Comprehensive Employment and Training Act of 1973. CETA legislation, representing as it does the culmination of years of trials and program efforts in manpower development, including employment creation and work-related education, will be examined in the final chapter.

Job Redesign and Enrichment for
Actualization in Work

In recent years there has been a marked increase in efforts to redesign work and enrich jobs, in order to reduce dissatisfaction and provide workers more opportunities for self-fulfillment or actualization through work. Quinn, Staines, and McCullough report over three thousand articles published on the topic of job satisfaction to date.[13] Dissatisfaction with work and jobs is said to lead to absenteeism, turnover, industrial sabotage, theft, alcoholism, drug use, shoddy products, and the general rootlessness that afflicts young workers in the United States. Terkel, after three years of interviewing hundreds of workers, reports: "For the many there is hardly concealed discontent."[14] Yankelovich, after surveying thousands of young workers, states that American society is in for a period of great stress in the next few years because of a working class that is dissatisfied and frustrated.[15] A *Boston Globe* series exploring what Massachusetts workers think about their jobs opens the concluding article in the series with this statement: "The problem: a lot of people hate their jobs. The solution: make the jobs better."[16]

A government report, *Work in America*, after asserting that dull, repetitive, and seemingly meaningless tasks offer little challenge or autonomy and cause discontent among workers at all occupational levels, recommends that jobs be redesigned, that self-renewal programs prepare workers for new jobs and equip them with additional training.[17] In congressional response, Senate Bill 736, "Worker Alienation Research and Technical Assistance Act of 1973," catalogues ills such as reduced productivity and poor quality workmanship, attributes these and other social and health ailments to alienation, and recommends research, pilot programs, and technical assistance to humanize working conditions and increase job satisfaction.

There are counterviews to these alarums and proposals. Kaplan, writing in the *Monthly Labor Review*, states: "Considerable sociological evidence indicates that many people do *not* seek greater opportunities for creativity and responsibility in their jobs."[18] Kaplan points out that many workers have a tolerance for the dull and repetitive, and even meaningless, tasks that some commentators might find unbearable. A series of seven national surveys and eight public-opinion polls conducted between 1958 and 1973 suggests that there has been no substantial change in overall levels of job satisfaction over the last decade. Quinn, Staines, and McCullough, in summarizing these surveys, conclude that job dissatisfaction does not appear to be increasing.[19] Though younger workers are less satisfied with their jobs than older workers, the same was true ten years ago. Nevertheless, the very volume of attention that the subject is receiving suggests both a problem and the likelihood of considerable attention to it in the years ahead.

The major share of responsibility for remediation of the situation will have to come through efforts in private industry, whatever the position of government-sponsored legislation and programs. *Work in America* reports on thirty developmental level programs for restructuring work and jobs, and in some cases the industrial process itself.[20] Companies have established job-enrichment and job-enlargement programs to provide workers with more responsible, interesting, and meaningful work.

Various underlying causes of dissatisfaction exist. What provokes one worker may please another, and vice versa. No simple design, specific set of steps for restructuring the situation, or organizational form of education or training serves to fit all the various job and work problems. Sometimes rather straightforward arrangements, offering more flexible work or production schedules or shortened work hours, suffice. Altered compensation and rate bases may alleviate some problems. Often the cause is psychic dissatisfaction, which must be diagnosed through group sessions under skilled and sensitive organizational behaviorists and training specialists. The work process may have to be modified into fewer fragmented and isolated steps. Workers may have to be given responsibility for carrying out more steps and participating in a more meaningful segment of work which will yield a more identifiable product or result. Patterns of supervision may have to be changed, and larger responsibility and decision powers allotted to workers. There is often an attempt to establish a team spirit and sense of camaraderie among work groups who as a team take responsibility for a complete process. Sometimes workers are merely provided with an overview of a large and complex industrial process so that they can place their own contributions in some meaningful context. Workers may also participate in discussion and creation of broad company goals and policies.

Many of the programs are small and cover only a few workers in selected jobs or departments of a firm, but others are extensive. The *Globe* series reports on a program covering 100,000 workers in twenty-three companies of the Bell System.[21] This program dates back to 1965, and the record provides a fair history of trial and success. Examples of job enrichment include letting correspondents draft replies rather than merely dispatching form letters, changing assembly processes from sets of many discrete tasks to be performed by individuals to more comprehensive segments of work performed by teams, and providing workers with an overview of the whole flow of a large and complex process. Prudential Insurance Company of Boston reorganized field offices for team responses, in order to give members both specialist status and also a generalist experience with the work flow. Some companies have organized special sections that act within their own firms as consultants on the redesign and enrichment of work. These consultants respond to requests by departments and divisions within the firm, organize group sessions to identify problems that cause dissatisfaction, and then organize joint responses for the solution of the problems identified. The process is apparently a continuing one, with the necessity of constant attention and correction of procedures. Consultant teams attempt to draw from worker groups both the identification of the problems and suggestions for solution. There is no set form of remediation.

If job- and work-design programs continue to develop, a new and important field of work-related education and training will have to develop to respond to rapidly changing conditions of work. In addition to diagnosis and redesign of work and jobs there will have to be continuing education and training, so workers can learn new jobs, supervisors acquire new behaviors and responses, and most important of all so that a learning ambience is created in which problems that arise in the future can be resolved through self-initiated efforts for remediation. There is as yet no lengthy history of experience in such efforts, either in the United States or other countries. In Figure 4-1 (p. 86) the "Actualization" segment is still fairly empty of specific program response possibilities. In the future it is likely that most new developments in work-related education will come in this area. It is difficult to determine whether or not depressed times and slow economic growth in the developed countries, and the ever-present pressure of poverty in the developing countries, will reduce concern with human relation programs that go beyond the production-efficiency and cost-effectiveness approaches developed in industries over the past century. The possibility of reduced concern for human satisfaction through work, when times are hard, will be examined in the section on future development in work-related education.

A Note on Work-Related Education
in Other Countries

Over the years many other countries have developed approaches designed to relate education more effectively to work. China, where once the mandarin was trained to rule through the most general study of art and moral philosophy and selected for the post on the basis of producing the eight-legged essay, has pioneered in the modern period with radical educational reforms designed to base schooling on work requirements. Reform periods have been intermittent, however, and interspersed with reversion to more formal academic patterns. Many of these reforms built work and production experience, as well as social action and political activity, into education programs for cadres and the masses. Lu Ting-yi quotes Mao's pronouncement in 1934 that it is Party Policy to combine education with productive labor.[22] In the Yenan period, partly out of necessity and under military and economic pressure, this policy was incorporated into practice in schools and training programs under Party control. The policy was re-stated and the practice intermittently implemented (Lu's policy statement was issued in 1958) over the years and down to the present time.

The Chinese Reform experience, as analyzed by Seybolt[23] in the Yenan period, and Munro[24] and Fraser[25] after 1950, reveals the difficulty of sustaining radical departures from formal schooling, even in a highly mobilized society directed by a strong and popular government. Munro details the ups and downs of educational reformations and counter reformations in China: the toleration of Western liberal arts models in higher education from 1949 to 1951; the adoption of technical manpower development schemes similar to Russian planning during the period 1952-1958; the egalitarian and work-based schooling of the Great Leap Period; a return to modification of the Russian approach from 1961 to 1964; and the blending of work and production with schooling during the Great Proletarian Cultural Revolution, and subsequently.

Seybolt describes the development of cadre and mass training around Yenan. In the fourth class at K'angta students were introduced to combined work and study in the school program. In part this work experience, primarily in food production, storage, and marketing was born of economic necessity, but it furnished a trial base for later, more systematic attempts to combine work and schooling. Later, as Seybolt states, "Productive labor by students would be considered absolutely requisite for attaining the Communist goals of eliminating the difference between mental and physical work."[26] Seybolt states that work/education was a desultory practice in 1939, and the pedagogical and political principles were not explicitly stated; nor did the principles last. In

1958, work/education was reintroduced during the Great Leap Forward, "as if no one had ever heard of it, much less practiced it. The same phenomenon recurred as an aspect of the Great Proletarian Cultural Revolution following retrenchment in academic education."[27]

Lu summed up the purposes of education: "Education must serve politics, must be combined with productive labor, and must be led by the Party."[28] Education combined with productive labor served political and economic ends. Labor leveled the class differences that formal schooling created. In tight circumstances all productive contributions counted, and, by paying for itself in part, schooling could accommodate larger numbers. Hence political, social and economic aims blended in work education.

Work-based education also served pedagogical ends, as the slogan "study what you do" indicates. Worker-learners were instructed to study their jobs and to improve performance by research into their work assignments. The curriculum became one in which the work, the job, and the job performance were the essential content for study, and the blending of work and study was close to complete and indivisible. This high water mark in the theory and practice of work education was attained prior to 1940 and followed by intermittent reversion back to more formal schooling models, described by Munro, Seybolt and Fraser.

If the history of reforms incorporating blends of schooling, work and production is uneven in China, results have been even more transient in other countries. Russia has moved through various mixes of production work and schooling. The factory schools, admired by John Dewey in the twenties, gradually became more like schools and less like factories; but there has always been a continuing blend of work and study, and workers' schools and correspondence programs for workers have always been a strong feature of Russian education. Europe has pioneered in apprenticeship programs, combining work and formal schooling; but the preferred model has always been the academy or gymnasium for those who were privileged to make it. The Latin American countries pioneered national apprenticeship programs, SENAI in Brazil, INCE in Venezuela, and SENA in Colombia, but these had only slight connection to the formal schools which represented the main line of educational effort.

In the Colombian SENA program the small numbers of graduates, highly selected through attrition and well trained, apparently do find employment and earn more than graduates from academic programs, at least in the early work years;[29] but the evidence does not clearly suggest that this advantage is lasting, or attributable uniquely to the program. Selectivity plays a strong part in results.

The national apprenticeship program model does indicate some unique potential for developing countries just beginning to expand employment in the modern sector industry. Enrollments in vocational and technical agricultural programs have just begun to grow in recent years, but early signs are that this area has promising possibilities for expansion. The programs do not offer any general formula for success, however. Whereas in Colombia about half of the firms sponsoring apprenticeship programs under the law absorb their graduates, in India, in the state of West Bengal, where industrial growth has stagnated in recent years, over a three-year period (1970-73), no graduates were hired in the firms that trained them.[30] Unemployment was close to 40 percent of graduates in their first three years out of the program. Nor do the numbers trained in national programs represent any significant portion of the age group populations that might need training. Nor, if Puryear's data on background of participants are representative, does the national apprenticeship service reach large numbers of clients from poorer and more deprived groups.[31]

National apprenticeship models are worth including in Figure 4-1 as a policy or program option; but in the United States, movement toward this form of organization of work-related education is unlikely. Over the years in the US, only in times of mobilization, as in World War II, has there been anything similar to the national apprenticeship service approach. Though there is national legislation governing standards (the National Apprenticeship Act or Fitzgerald Act of 1937), the initiative is carried largely on a voluntary basis by private firms of size. Still, national apprentice-training programs did sometimes blend academic and vocational training for secondary-school-age groups; and sometimes the training programs were production-based.

In India, Gandhi through the *nai talim* (new education) sought to make primary schools production based. The children were to use the *takli* and the *charkha* (spinning frame and wheel), not only to produce cloth and to earn, and not only to acquire work skills, but also to apply academic studies to solution of practical problems and to apply practical experience to inform and concretize academic knowledge. At the level of theory, at any rate, this was one of the most complete blendings of production, skill training, and academic learning. In the *nai talim* approach, school production units turned out a product of economic value in a poor country, fostered cottage industries, and preserved traditional skills; and as self-supporting production units, the schools, as Gandhi envisaged it, would not have to depend on revenues raised by the British rulers through taxes on alcoholic beverages. This source of revenue was held to be evil, and production-based schools were a way of avoiding dependence on evil. This was not the central notion of *nai talim*, which had many objectives. Incorporated as an official program, called "Basic Education" after independence, *nai talim* ended as an economic and pedagogical travesty of the original notions. Basic Education has gradually expired and been buried in the highly formal primary schooling of the various states of India. There is talk of reviving work/education at a higher level, and in the length and breadth and variety of India there are many innovative work/education programs, but the general pattern is unrelievedly formal and academic.

In capitalist or communist countries the use of production situations and work experience as a supplement and sometimes a substitute for classroom study is widespread. The history of work and production-based education trials is long; attempts have been widespread, and ideological and political backing runs a very broad spectrum.

A review of the history of work-related education in the United States, and a brief look at comparative experience in other countries, suggest that there is a range of possibilities for combining education and training with work experience. Figure 4-1 attempts to summarize these and group them according to whether the aim is to prepare people to enter work, retrain workers in order to adapt them for new jobs, or redesign work itself to provide more self-actualization and psychic return.

The next chapter will trace program response possibilities appropriate for the fifteen-year employment and educational forecast presented in the previous chapter.

4

A Policy and Program Schema for Responding to Education and Employment Needs

Introduction

Figure 4-1 attempts to relate education and training programs to work, job, and career development, and more generally to employment policies. In discussing Figure 4-1 only passing comment will be made on general employment policies, in order to concentrate on work-related education and training programs designed to respond to employment opportunities created. Still, without some attention to policies and programs to create employment, no discussion of education and training for employment suffices.

Work-related education and training programs include programs to prepare workers for entry into work, programs to assist workers to adapt to changed job or work requirements, and programs for providing enhanced material and psychic returns from work. Much less is known about the latter kind of program, for the history of attempts to redesign and enrich work and jobs is short, and efforts are only beginning. An alternative to work redesign to provide increased satisfaction from work is mobilization around an ideology which provides compensatory satisfaction that goes beyond the work or job situation. Since mobilization on an ideological base is not a significant feature of the U.S. situation, as opposed to China for example, the mobilization alternative will not be dealt with in detail.

In addition to education and training programs for preparation, adaptation, and actualization in work, the schema in Figure 4-1 also indicates that supporting services such as guidance, placement, and health and work counseling assistance are necessary, especially for groups handicapped by physical disabilities or through past economic and social deprivation.

Figure 4-1 is a schema and just that. It merely attempts to array policies and program response possibilities in some kind of single sketch. It is not a model in the sense that relationships among programs and among policies and programs are specified. Much less does it have any dynamic or attempt to portray the effects of changes in program elements and the relationship among them over time.

A Brief Note on Employment Policies

During the forecast period it is reasonable to assume that policies will be directed toward full employment, as this is now defined, i.e. employment for

85

PREPARATION

[basic academic schooling
[career exploration
pre-vocational training
institutional, vocational, industrial, technical
  education
work sample
school based production simulation
school based production
pre-apprenticeship (remedial, outreach, COP)
pre-work remedial
cooperative programs
work-study programs

ADAPTATION

skill center (school based/industry related;
  cluster, multioccupational, training)
skill center (industry based/school related
  training and retraining)
apprenticeship (national programs)
apprenticeship (single industry)
[dispersed worksites (unpaid real jobs)
[home industry (crafts)
work crews (dispersed, controlled profit)
contract/project service (for profit, with training)
[controlled, supervised employment
sheltered shops
vestibule job (support)
other programs for institutionalized & handicapped
  └ (government/institutional marketing)
on-job training/re-training (formal)
on-job training (informal)
on-job training (incidental spin-off)
youth mobilization for service

ACTUALIZATION

job development, new careers, public sector
small industry & service enterprise
  development for self-employment
job restructuring (organizational setting)
[restructuring (upgrading work, job enrichment)
[restructuring/upgrading workers
productivity training
participation training
leadership training
[continuing education
[career development

UNEXPLORED

ADAPTATION/PREPARATION
preparation for retirement, leisure, death.

UNEXPLORED

GUIDANCE
PLACEMENT
SUPPORT

POLICY BASES FOR
EMPLOYMENT CREATION

Government Plans & Policies Create
  Conditions to Maximize Em-
  ployment:
Monetary/Fiscal, Tax & Transfer,
  Credit, Investment, Encourage
  Medium Technology, Labor Intensive
  (Construction, Land Tenure &
  Agricultural Credit)

Private Sector Invests, Expands
  Production
1) Industry—More Plants, Equipment,
  More Shifts, Etc.
2) Agriculture—More Land Farmed,
  More Crops Per Year Per Area
3) Service—More Customers From 1 &
  2.
1, 2, 3, etc. Creates Jobs

Government Creates Work & Jobs
  Directly

Public Spending:
1) Large Public Works for Development
  and Employment
2) Hiring in Public Sector Enterprises
3) Increase Social Services (Education,
  Health, Welfare)
4) Youth Mobilization (Collective,
  Military, CCC, NYA, etc.)

Figure 4-1: A Schema of Work-Related Education Programs in the United States.

about 95 percent of the labor force. Bureau of Labor Statistics projections assume that unemployment will be held somewhere around 4 percent, with intervention at national and local level, and remedial action when the rates fluctuate much beyond this level. This is not total employment, nor given the inflationary consequences does it seem that total employment will be a likely policy goal in the near future. Maintaining employment near the 95 percent level currently seems to be an almost unattainable goal. Given the economic growth forecast and diminished growth in the labor force, anything approaching a full-employment policy cannot even be envisaged, unless there is a policy of recurrent intervention, backed up by programs maintained in constant readiness to support such interventions. In fact, given the situation in 1975, with unemployment above 8 percent nationally and climbing, during the entire forecast period the economy may never reach a 4 percent unemployment base. This does not invalidate the general analysis underlying the Bureau of Labor Statistics projections of the policy and program consequences traced from it. Quite the contrary; it makes the recommendations for employment-directed policies and work-related education programs all the more significant, a point that is constantly repeated in this book.

Figure 4-1 lists some of the policy and program possibilities for stimulating the economy and generating employment, and only cursory attention can be given to such matters here. Modification of tax and revenue measures, increases of transfers and subsidies, modification of credit rates, reserves, and government bond transactions, and public spending for new facilities and services are fiscal and monetary policies that may be used to stimulate the economy. Direct generation of employment is provided through public employment programs and manpower-development programs.

Manpower development through education, training, job placement, and worker-supporting services has been a response to employment development and maintenance in the United States. The effect of such programs on a free-standing basis, unaccompanied or preceded by appropriate monetary and fiscal policies for stimulating the economy, is limited, but during past periods of economic growth there has been strong support for manpower development through education and training. These efforts are seemingly more positive and palatable than direct employment creation, especially through public employment programs; but they are no substitute when the need is acute. In recent periods of general economic growth the view prevailed that employment problems were temporary and local imbalances, and that providing skilled workers who were in short supply in a given region or economic activity would stimulate industrial expansion and employment creation. Better matching of skilled workers to job openings in shortage areas was judged to be an adequate response to sustain increased economic activity.

To support the manpower-training response, there must be current labor-market information and the matching of demand and supply through employment-service activity. In the current depression with high general unemployment, partial manpower-training responses are clearly inadequate. The demand for labor is generally low and unemployment high, even for skilled workers and highly trained professionals and technicians. Employment must be stimulated, and in some cases created. Though the government is moving, albeit slowly with monetary and fiscal policies, easing credit, cutting taxes, offering concessions to business investment, it has not yet moved in any significant or direct effort to create employment. Current public service employment programs will not create enough jobs even to be reflected in the national employment rates. In some cases new jobs will merely be filled by employees cut from current state and local government payrolls because of depressed times and reduced revenues. New employment is not created, only the source of funding to support the jobs is changed.

Manpower development through education and training is not an adequate response to present unemployment and in a future of slow economic growth and lagging employment the problem may continue even after there is a decline from present high levels of unemployment. Employment creation and job development will have to accompany future training programs, and the likelihood is that the entire range of policies and programs from monetary and fiscal to public employment will be needed.

In the US, monetary and fiscal policies to stimulate and maintain growth in the economy have been the basic means to increase or maintain employment. The present response to high employment indicates that this will continue to be the case in future years. In the developing countries more direct measures to expand employment in private and public sector enterprises have also included investment priorities for labor-using projects and enterprises, encouragement of intermediate, labor-using technology, encouragement of multiple shifts in existing plants, and direct action through large-scale public employment projects. These approaches may now seem less remote from US needs, and the future may make them more likely prospects. Public employment programs are large and almost a continuous necessity in India, where growth lags and new entrants into the work force vastly exceed the number of new jobs and full-time employment possibilities that develop outside of agriculture. Development economists generally have not favored direct employment policies for low-income countries, and most development models are investment based, aiming to maximize growth of output through savings, investment, and improved capital/output relationships, with employment a by-product of growth maximization. In the US public employment programs are maintained at a reduced level, with a provision for expansion if the situation warrants. Current indications are that expansion is not accomplished easily or quickly when unemployment suddenly rises.

The situation may well warrant expansion over the coming fifteen-year period, and direct public employment programs such as PEP, and other indirect programs such as Operation Mainstream, may be expanded over the period under

CETA (Comprehensive Employment and Training Act of 1973) or through follow-on amendments. Though the early years of the forecast do not indicate proportionately large numbers of young people to be accommodated, cohorts are still sizable, given the present small numbers in such programs. Programs for older workers are even smaller and less well developed, and this may be a severe shortcoming of existing policies and programs.

Table 2-21 (p. 60) indicates that very small numbers are accomodated in all of the special employment/training programs. The numbers enrolled in the Public Employment Program (PEP), JOBS, Neighborhood Youth Corps, Operation Mainstream, and Public Service Careers seem to have fallen over the three-year period 1972-1974.[1] According to the legislative provisions of the Comprehensive Employment and Training Act (CETA) of 1973, reduced program coverage will be compensated for by increased accommodation under the new comprehensive manpower services provided in Title I. The underlying approach of CETA, both in its comprehensive manpower services and other titles, is to shift major responsibility for program operation to state and local cooperating bodies. This is also the approach embodied in public employment programs as they are expanded to meet current unemployment. Presumably, job creation programs that are designed and managed according to local needs will be more responsive to participant needs and more productive in works accomplished.

In any case, public employment programs offering middle-level jobs, and even the provision of mass, low-skilled employment at low wages, are likely in the slow growth years ahead. With smaller cohorts of young people, program developments are not likely to be confined to youth mobilization, in the old pattern of the Civilian Conservation Corps, but more likely to be designed for workers of mature years and higher skills and experience, as in some of the more specialized programs of the Works Progress Administration.

Several small and temporary programs of recent years may provide good pilot models for the future, inasmuch as they have dealt with older workers and in some cases skilled and educated participants. Operation Mainstream, a small program for older workers, has been mentioned. This may be an important model for providing gainful and, if possible, meaningful, employment for older citizens with low educational qualifications who are nearing, but will not have reached, retirement by the middle of the period. Projections of educational attainment in the labor force indicate that there will be 10 million workers with less than eight grades of schooling in 1980, and this will not drop to 6 million until 1990. Unemployment for this relatively small group could still be painful, and programs must be developed accordingly. Though training and retraining may be important components, the central feature should be provision of jobs.

Programs for the disadvantaged and less educated may also develop under NMWP, the National Migrant Workers Program, to serve workers with severe language as well as other handicaps.

For the better educated, a more likely model might be TMRP, the Technology Mobilization and Reemployment Program, which helped highly trained scientists and engineers by providing retraining and placement and support services after the large cutbacks in space and defense programs. These workers were older (almost half were forty-five); better educated (almost 60 percent engineers); and higher salaried in their previous employ—almost 82 percent earned ten thousand dollars or more a year. The future will require more than a repeat run of TMRP, however, for the problem will not be so much one of providing assistance in job placement in a still growing economy, but one of creating jobs in a sluggish economy. Nor will it be a matter of providing entry-level or low-skilled jobs, but of providing employment at a level of challenge and reward that is not demeaning to participants. There will be a need for job creation and job enrichment and training and job restructuring that are, in terms of Figure 4-1, both adaptive and developmental or actualizing.

The provision of employment in specially affected sectors of economic activity may be modeled on the Technology Mobilization and Reemployment Program, or designed to provide special necessary services as in Public Employment Program (PEP). In general, the very severe problems of older workers may require attention under a variety of legislative approaches, including future expansion and improvement of the OAA, the Older Americans Act.

A future free of war, or at least wars fought by large draft naval and ground forces, may shrink the requirements for veterans' adjustment and training programs and for demobilization, training programs, and job placement for the military personnel—e.g., transition, worker outflow from a professionalized military service, may be handled in more comprehensive manpower programs—and it is likely that the services may also provide fewer trained personnel for the civilian labor force. In some years the military provided skill and technical training for half a million men, and this burden will have to be assumed by some other agency if there are to be smaller forces and fewer exits into civilian jobs. Also, jobs once provided by the military itself may have to be provided through other programs.

In summary, now and continuing in the years ahead, direct and indirect measures to create jobs and enhance employment opportunity will have to be designed and supported so as to cover almost all age ranges, varying levels of educational attainment, and a variety of special needs. Population groups with special needs include the handicapped and disadvantaged, who require a variety of supporting services, such as guidance, placement, follow-up support, counseling health services, and in some cases, the structured transition to employment furnished by vestibular arrangements and sheltered shops.

Monetary and fiscal policies for stimulating employment, and direct employment creation, or maintenance programs, run under government auspices have been briefly treated only to provide an outline of the program and policy schema. The main object is to examine the gamut of program possibilities for fitting education and training to employment that will be the end result of other policy measures.

Employment-Directed Education and Training

Over the past fifteen years a great variety of innovative program approaches to manpower development and training have been initiated. Legislation directed toward general manpower development, enhancement of economic opportunity, especially for the disadvantaged, and expansion and improvement of employment-directed education and training has provided a trial basis for the vast array of program responses depicted in Figure 4-1. Major lines of development came out of the Manpower Development and Training Act of 1962, the Vocational Education Act of 1963, the Economic Opportunity Act of 1964, the 1968 amendments to the Vocational Education Act, general Office of Education program initiatives and the Education amendments of 1972 directed toward career education, the Comprehensive Manpower Program of 1972, and the successor Comprehensive Employment and Training Act of 1973. Agencies of the Department of Labor, Health, Education and Welfare, and the Office of Economic Opportunity, sometimes in partnership, and often independently, and supported by state, community, and private agencies, have designed and developed an array of institutional, job-based and combined school-and-on-job experience that provide a base sufficient for most future education and training needs.

The need to provide training and support services to client groups never before served called forth ingenious yet effective program response by both public and private agencies. The immediate future is not likely to bring forth any new client groups or needs that have not been experienced in the immediate past. A rich record of success and failure has been written, and the great need ahead is to profit from it. Some groups, particularly in the older age ranges, have been served imperfectly or incompletely, but there is some experience with every ethnic group, age group, educational level, sex, and geographic area clientele. In fact, except for a few gaps that will be noted, the need for the immediate future is not so much for innovative initiatives serving undiscovered client groups as it is for rationalization of the many and complex program possibilities that have already been tried, evaluation of the results, and improvement and expansion of programs to make them more comprehensive and cost-effective at appropriate scale.

In Figure 4-1 programs are arrayed under the three headings "preparation," "adaptation," and "actualization." Programs in the preparation segment are mainly the conventional general-education and vocational-training programs offered in school settings, from primary school to postsecondary level. The objective of such programs is to prepare participants, usually for entry-level jobs.

Programs in the adaptation segment are more often run outside of formal school settings, sometimes in centers or programs that connect classroom and work site, or wholly in the industry or on the job site. The programs may prepare for entry-level jobs, or for moving from one job skill or occupation to another. Both preparational and adaptive programs require guidance, placement, and job-support services. Even apprenticeship and on-job training programs may require placement services for locating the participant in regular employment after completion of the training.

Some of the programs in the adaptive segment may require work/training coordinators to locate work and training opportunities and to coordinate the two for best effect. This would also be true of work/study programs based in school. Both preparational and adaptive programs designed to serve handicapped and disadvantaged groups depend heavily on strong and continuing supportive services in addition to training. In general, in the immediate past, most innovative effort has come in the development of new forms of adaptive programs that entail bringing training and work site closer together.

There have been some advances in research and development to support the preparation segment, however, notably through the rationalization of job and training requirements through job-cluster analysis. Job-cluster analysis attempts to determine in precise terms the differences and similarities in the performance requirements of occupations. It permits structuring jobs in groups according to common elements or requirements. This permits more efficient training programs, in that groups from related occupations can be trained together in those performance requirements which are common, and only the different requirements would entail separate training. More important, the identification of relationships among occupations, based on common requirements, provides a basis for planning career development through mobility from one related job to another at a coordinate level, or for developing job ladders so that a student or worker can plan career lines from jobs at lower to higher levels. Clusters also reveal fundamental patterns of requirements in jobs and careers, and hence the job cluster or family is an essential support for providing a general perspective of the world of work across several different occupations.

Cluster research can support programs in career education that feature earlier familiarization with the world of work in the lower grades and combination of work and educational experience through cooperative and work study programs in the higher grades. At the postsecondary level, work-related preparational programs in junior colleges and institutes have shown considerable innovation and promise.

Future program trends are likely to continue on these lines, supported by advances in instructional technology. Classroom study and work on site will be joined, bringing a considerable increase in the flexibility of programs. Education and training experience can be interspersed with intervening periods of work. If the future indicates one thing, it is that the job and work may become more prized and the school place less so in times of job scarcity; but the long-run prospect is not usurpation of traditional turf, but an exchange in which the school acquires action and disciplined purpose from the work site, and work acquires some of the open-ended promise and anticipation that education offers when it is good.

The third program segment, actualization, covers the creation or reshaping of work opportunities, which go beyond obtaining and holding a job, to include improvement of the work and job situation through job redesign, restructuring, and enrichment, the development of the worker through training and improvement programs, and the combination of job and worker improvement designed to provide a work lifetime of career satisfaction. The training portion of this segment may be carried on in formal classroom settings through continuing education, or through in-service development, or through a combination of the two.

There has been the least experience in the design, development, and implementation of actualization programs, and as Figure 4-1 indicates, at the upper levels the possibilities of this segment are still relatively unexplored. Job-restructuring and -enrichment programs in organized industry are still few and scattered and with relatively few years of trial behind them in the United States, although the thirty or more programs described in *Work in America* have had fair success when measured in economic, psychic, and social return.[2] Attempts to create new and satisfying professional opportunities, especially in emerging fields, have had some limited trial in recent times. There has been longer and more varied experience with training designed to improve productivity and leadership, and less for participation, job satisfaction, and self-realization through work. Organizational behavior clinicians have a repertory of approaches for training for productivity, leadership, participation, and, in fewer instances, career satisfaction. Private firms have made substantial investment in continuing-education programs to contribute to the general development of their managers and officials.

Beyond career-development programs lie possibilities that have yet to be explored. Training and counseling designed to assist the transition from active work to semiretirement, full-retirement, and leisure are receiving current attention, and with a work force that is aging in the years ahead this is an area that will be developed. With jobs in scarce supply, especially for educated young people entering the work force, there may have to be job- and work-rationing schemes leading to reduced work days and weeks and earlier retirement. Older workers will require education and training to adapt to these situations creatively and productively. This segment of program possibilities has not had lengthy or systematic attention during the years when concern for economic opportunity for youth and the disadvantaged has claimed major attention and a major share of resources and innovative program development. In the future there will be increased attention, and hopefully corresponding investment, in developing this segment of education and training for work and combinations of work and leisure. One main line of development will center on restructuring the job and work situation itself, and another on helping workers attain increased satisfaction and fulfillment in their work and leisure.

Inasmuch as there are no single causes for worker or student dissatisfaction of the kind Terkel,[3] Rosak,[4] and the Task Force on Work in America[5] document, there can be no single approach to the problem. Raising earnings and enhancing work conditions are obvious approaches, but there are other needs. For those seeking increased autonomy and independence, there may have to be assistance in starting and running small enterprises for self-employment; for those who are fulfilled by participating in a process that results in a tangible final product, technology and production scheduling may have to be modified, and fabrication and assembly procedures changed; for those rewarded by social and humane service, increased service programs may have to be supported; for those who wish to share in policy and planning, management and decision processes may have to be modified, participation broadened, and team approaches devised; for those who work in spurts and at odd hours, schedules may have to be made more flexible.

For career-education programs of the future, the objective at the preparation stage may be to help individuals not so much in exploring occupations and their requirements, as in identification of their own goals and the work styles and rewards that best fit them. At the adaptation stage the object may be to help individuals fit their goals and styles to the requirements of the work situation; and at the actualization stage the aim may be to help make the best adaptation of the work to the worker's style and goals. At the moment it is not simply a matter of devising and implementing programs for this last objective; even the approach to researching the underlying questions is not clear. If it is established that worker dissatisfaction is widespread, research still must establish the major typologies or categories of dissatisfaction, the extent to which it is lasting and serious, the possible responses to work redesign and their costs. Then the major research and development task for career education is development of programs to respond to the underlying conditions that analysis reveals.

Preparation

Introduction. The program possibilities in this segment fan out from basic academic schooling, long the major claimant on public and private attention and resources, to more recent and less traditional approaches. Public, familial, and individual priorities are not likely to shift away from formal schooling over the next fifteen years, but the reduced enrollment burdens over the first half of the period will permit attention and resources to be directed to other program possibilities. A much stronger career exploration and development program may be one possibility, permitting earlier and more intensive introduction to personal exploration of work styles and goals, general job, work, and career information and orientation, and a more comprehensive view of alternative career trajectories possible in the future.

With smaller numbers, and more openness and flexibility, this should permit linking both general and vocational schooling with production situations and social and cultural enterprises outside the classroom. The discipline and reality of production work, "the action," can be brought into the school in simulated and actual form, through work sample methods, production simulation, and student-managed production enterprises based in the school. Students can experience the classroom and the job through cooperative programs and work/study opportunities. Cooperative education programs, as described by Evans, Mangum, and Pragan,[6] are those in which the students work part-time and attend school part-time; and the central purpose is to provide a meaningful work experience combined with formal education, in order to develop work-related knowledge, skills, and attitudes. Work/study programs serve primarily to aid needy students, by providing earnings for jobs mainly in public agencies. Other terms used for combined work and study are "experienced-based education," "work-based education," "work education," "employment-based education," and sometimes the broader term "career education." The essential feature of work-related education is a combination of work and formal schooling that permits earning and learning, work experience and sometimes training.

The combination of work and study is not likely to be less needed in the future, particularly as more older participants, primarily job-based rather than school-based, are eligible for participation. The opening of schooling to work and job experience will not be a one-way exchange, for as the disciplined orientation of work and production enters the school, the open-ended promise of study and intellectual exploration will go the other way. Presently such program opportunities exist, but the future should permit:

1. A marked expansion of coverage so that more than the present small number of students can participate. Coverage is minimal, even in urban, industrial, and commercial centers.

2. Expansion of coverage to areas where thin populations and light economic activity offer few opportunities for school-industry arrangements. Regionalization of work/study opportunities may have to be supported with the construction of boarding facilities in centers, provision of transportation, or development of work-experience camps. Home- and farm-based programs served by mobile teams or through the media are also possibilities. Trial response to the outreach problem will be discussed in the pages immediately following.

3. Expansion of opportunities into more fields, and into low-level and dead-end jobs. Case studies of fifty work-education-program sites indicate a very heavy concentration in a few service and commercial fields, and almost no entry job experience in other more interesting and developmental opportunities.[7]

There are large numbers of programs where students perform menial service and clerical tasks in small stores, restaurants, and public institutions; few of these situations offer anything but the meanest perspective on the world of work, with little relevance to career development and slim prospects for advancement. Many of the programs seem to be made up after the fact and on the basis of circumstances, with students getting their own after-hours jobs, in the traditional part-time work open to them. To this is added a program façade of school recognition and credit built up to fit the existing situation. Study of work-education programs indicated only a few situations where there is any possibility of the job contributing to career development. In fact, some of the situations are so mean that they could only inspire work avoidance in young people of any sense or sensibility. Work education as it now goes on in many of the most conventional situations may actually be counterproductive for job and career development.

Improving School-Work Programs. A heavy investment in improvement of job and program development and coordination will be required if the work/study movement is to develop beyond the present primitive stage it is in. This will require:

1. Concentrating more program support for cooperative arrangements between postsecondary-level training programs and work opportunities. Work/ study and cooperative arrangements revealed in the fifty case studies were much more interesting at the postsecondary level.[8] This merely reflects the reality that there is less resistance to hiring, even on a cooperative or work/study basis, older students from higher-level technical training institutions. It is also part of a general drift in many states to push formal technical and occupational training up beyond the secondary school to junior colleges and technical-training institutes. This upward movement will and should continue. Policy and program response should be so developed.

Movement upward does not solve the problem of serving large numbers of students who will never reach the postsecondary level, particularly without some realistic occupational experience and earning as a holding device during the long years of formal schooling. Primary responsibility for vocational/technical education has been centered at different levels in different states. In Washington, Oregon, California, Illinois, Texas, and Maine the primary responsibility is at postsecondary level; whereas in Massachusetts, Maryland, New York, Ohio, Virginia, South Carolina, Colorado, Georgia, Kansas, Florida, Pennsylvania, and Wisconsin the primary agency for vocational/technical education is at secondary level. Though current thought seems to favor moving the responsibility for skill training toward postsecondary and using secondary level for basic preparation and exploration, no clearly demonstrable advantage is yet shown.

There are first-rate programs in states where the responsibility is divided between both levels. Testing the relative merit would be difficult, inasmuch as the payoff is different under each pattern. At the secondary level there is less likelihood of losing those who might not survive to postsecondary, and hence more likelihood of serving the disadvantaged in formal school programs. On the other hand, postsecondary-level programs are generally more successful when placement records and earnings of graduates are used as the criteria. If the future brings decreased emphasis on more and more formal schooling, it may be well to have secondary-level opportunities available in some institutions in states where there are large numbers of disadvantaged youth. If this clientele declines, hopefully, programs can be moved up.

2. Permitting heavier subsidies to enterprises where jobs and training can be developed. Exploitation and profiteering are possible, but if work experience is as valuable as commentators say it is, the opportunity for experience will have to be paid for. It seems naïve for program developers to expect that private businessmen will provide training and experience opportunities without appropriate incentives. What is more likely is that they will provide menial tasks at low pay, as is now the case. Conceptually, there should be no more difficulty in providing public funds for a work scholarship than for an academic scholarship. In fact, with job opportunities scarcer than study opportunities in the future, the provision of public money for work-training opportunities seems a more economic and politically attractive investment possibility than schooling. The whole matter must be researched and tried, and present restrictions that hem in the cooperative programs will have to be lifted and the whole approach broadened. All the usual questions that surround the provision of scholarship assistance, and a few problems that are unique, should be investigated; i.e., whether the money for the job opportunity should be paid to the institutions or directly to the enterprise, or in the form of a voucher to parent or participant; how much should be paid and whether the scale should vary according to the field of work and amount of training provided; what incentives would sweeten cooperation from unions and union members (payment of on-job training fees into union pension funds, etc.); what degree of choice the school, employer, worker/trainee should have; how selective the programs should be; whether small enterprises can be created or small business investment credit expanded to provide jobs in areas of scarcity; etc., etc.

3. Modifying union and licensing and legislative barriers when they are not directly designed to protect the health and safety of the trainees. Again this will not be accomplished without study, carefully planned arrangements, and incentives for changing present restrictions. With fewer jobs for union members, resistance to programs developed to expand work rolls will be formidable.

4. Training, retraining, and information programs for work-education co-ordinators. This is a new field with an exacting set of training and experience requirements. Many coordinators seem to have drifted into their assignments, fallen heir to them through default, or been appointed without demonstrating talent, interest, or training. The job itself has to be defined and training

programs developed accordingly. After training there must be informational support programs, retraining opportunities, and professional exchange. One important research-and-developmental task is a careful analysis of the requirements of the work-education coordinator's job, and the development of training programs and selection criteria for improving performance in the job.

5. Greater utilization of community support possibilities through community agencies, industrial and commercial groups, and local government officials outside of the school department. Program experience indicates only sporadic use of these possibilities. The community-development organizations, large multipurpose groupings of profit and nonprofit enterprises, should provide possibilities for sponsoring work and training programs combined.

6. Greater incorporation of the programs within the school-student social structure, with resulting participation of students and student groups in developing and running work-experience programs. In many situations the work/study and cooperative participants seem marginal to the social and academic and sports structures that predominately set school-community life style. Since much of the initiative seems to be carried by the individual student participants in any case, the main need is to recognize and exploit what is already a fact.

7. Establishing more formal relationships of work/study and cooperative programs to manpower-development and employment-support programs, so that the resources of the comprehensive employment programs can be used to support the school and work programs. Students holding part-time jobs make up over 50 percent of the labor force under twenty years old. There is no persuasive reason why the coverage capability of the 2500 employment centers around the country cannot be used to locate and develop work/study opportunities, particularly for older students at the postsecondary level.

8. Provision of centralized supporting services for work-related and cooperative education programs that go on at widely dispersed job and school sites. This is especially necessary, but especially difficult, in areas where industries and enterprises are small and scattered, and local school resources are inadequate to provide the testing, guidance, counseling, placement, and work coordination activities that are required for programs to succeed at any significant scale of participation. Trials of centralized support models for dispersed sites are going on, for example, under the experienced-based career-education programs supported by NIE, and exemplified in the programs around Charleston, West Virginia supported by the Appalachia Educational Laboratory. The experience of this trial tends to support the notion of the difficulty of expanding work-related education to areas where there are thin concentrations of population and economic activity. Costs tend to run high, and the programs tend to become overbalanced on demonstrating the academic, philosophical, and psychological returns, rather than economic and employment gains. Still, it is difficult to envisage work/study and cooperative education programs serving widely in rural areas without some form of regional support system.

9. Improvement of skill training in work-education programs. This is a problem that could plague the entire career-education movement. Quite apart from sporadic sniping from traditional vocational educators, who deplore the underemphasis on skill training, a future of leaner times and more competition for jobs may make skill training a necessity in any career-education or work-education program. It is fundamental to investigate how skill training can be a more important feature of work-education programs; or perhaps even *if* it can, in some situations. Skill training must be included somewhere in the school or work program or, career education will lack full utility. How training in at least one skill cluster can be made a part of every secondary-school program is a real problem for curriculum research for the future. Reserving the problem for on-the-job is a copout much loved by commentators.

Work education is important because it lies on the junction of preparation and adaptation. In future years the major development is likely to be an educational exchange from job back to school, as well as from school out to job, the participants being older workers primarily attempting to continue their education and at the same time protect their job tenure and earnings. Research-and-development activities must precede major program advances of this kind. Though there will in the future be some parallels with present predominating forms of programs which serve primarily school-age groups, there will be differences designed for service to older and more experienced work-based groups. Under MDTA training programs, and envisaged in the expansion of comprehensive manpower development programs, there are current efforts, though small, which serve clients more like the older groups that must be served in the future.

Adaptation

Skill Centers and Occupational Clusters. Just as work/study and cooperative-education programs could be shifted from the preparation to the adaptation segment—and this shift will come when the participants are older and primarily job based rather than school based—so the placement of skill-center programs in the adaptation segment is arbitrary. The original center models were halfway between institutionalized education and in-industry training, and fifty or more of these centers were operating under MDTA auspices in 1967. The centers, for example the Syracuse Center, served disadvantaged youth in a training environment that closely resembled the organized production situation of industry. A range of supporting services was also provided, and the pattern of supervision and production scheduling simulated the requirements of an industrial setting, with norms, standards, and job-order scheduling. At a later point basic and remedial general education were added to the center programs.

Centers can develop in the direction of a more institutionalized and school-based program, such as the Philadelphia Skill Center Project; or an in-industry operation where, as the program locus and the direction and control are more centered in industry, the enterprise begins to resemble an OJT (on-job training) or apprenticeship program. There is an important conceptual difference, however, centering on the multioccupational, cluster, or job/family approach that underlies program development in many skill centers. The aim is not so much to train for a specific or narrow skill or craft as to provide training that may fit several related occupational or production or service-activity requirements.

In recent years there has been considerable stress on job cluster analysis for the purpose of developing training clusters, families of occupations, for which common training can be given. The US Office of Education list of fifteen "occupational clusters,"[9] and the Philadelphia Skill Center modification of the OE list[10] provide examples of the cluster, family, or field approach. The rationale of the approach is persuasive. Given the large amount of interoccupational mobility in the labor force, the less-than-exact fit between training and occupation in manpower schema, and the rigidity of the old single craft, occupation, or skill training approach, the development of groupings in which single training programs can prepare for increased inter-occupational mobility has much to commend it. The clusters or groupings have been derived with various degrees of system and rigorous analysis. Levin and Martin[11] used a hierarchical grouping method devised by Ward[12] to group library and information-retrieval jobs. Wolf, Durstine, and Davis[13] applied a factor analysis to reduce and relate Dictionary of Occupational Titles jobs on a skill- and traits-required basis. Other lists of clusters seem to have been developed by guess and common sense. The lists appear to be no more than mixtures of occupations and economic activity groups, as if the International Standard Classification of Occupations was stirred in with the International Standard Industrial Classification of all Economic Activities. The difference between job-cluster and occupational-grouping systems reflects the fact that various approaches are required for varying purposes:

1. Providing a structure for a broad orientation to the world of work, in which case some mixture of occupational requirements and economic activity is required, as in the OE list.

2. Improving occupational groupings and training groupings so that the fit between manpower demand and supply are improved.

3. Deriving training-skill requirements from job-performance requirements in order to make skill-training programs both more responsive to occupational demand and more flexible in the face of the inevitable changes in job requirements and the need to train for mobility.

Providing a basis for 3 above is the most difficult and requires the greatest rigor, but even when rigorous analysis is applied, performance requirements in the real work situation change faster than training program responses. Clusters may rapidly become outmoded as jobs change. The market shifts, technology changes, and workers' job interests and opportunities change. Hence, there are alternatives to the cluster or grouping approach, although they may not seem as systematic or analytic.

Flexible and Piecewise Training. The alternative is simply to face the inevitability of change and the need to offer a partial response that can be spread over time as requirements shift. The underlying notion is recognition that no training program, no matter how logically it is designed and how comprehensive in coverage it purports to be, can turn out master workers adequately equipped for all future job requirements. Hence, training is offered in pieces and in response to immediate and narrow job requirements; and other pieces are added as markets shift and technology changes, and job requirements change.

This piecewise training is a closer simulation of the reality of how workers usually attain mastery of their jobs. It better fits shifts in product market and changes such shifts engender in job market requirements. Piecewise response also better fits shifts in technology that entail shifts in process, performance, and skill requirements. Flexible training may also better fit a future of employment-based education, in which the job dominates the schooling. In practical terms piecewise training may appear chaotic, as training programs must constantly change to meet changes in market and technology. Investment in shops, equipment, and tools have to be carefully planned and programs carefully designed to reduce waste. Program changes have their costs, however. Open/entry and open/exit for training periods of varying length make for difficult scheduling. Constant investment in market surveys are necessary to indicate needed shifts, as job markets saturate, new products require new processes, and new technologies require new combinations of skills.

Evidence deducible from learning theory suggests mixed returns for segmented and piecewise training. Though spaced practice, as opposed to the mass practice of conventional and more complete vocational programs, may have merit, and the constant contact with job reality may motivate more strongly, there is likely to be diminished possibilities of generalization and transfer of training. To accomplish transfer the program must be designed so that training segments and work experience segments are stitched together in some coherent scheme, and generalizations are explicitly drawn from both and used to shape instruction over time. Experience with such approaches by design rather than by accident are not common, though this is the underlying notion for the design and conduct of the Calcutta Youth Self-Employment Center (CYSEC).[14] The matter is discussed here merely to indicate that the cluster or family approach to job and training design is not the be-all and end-all in development of training programs that are more responsive to work and employment requirements. With a future of greater flexibility in open/entrance and open/exit training programs interspersed with work experience, and with older workers with a greater experiential background and higher general educational level the piecewise pattern may have more viability; but development of even fair-sized, much less systematic, research and evaluation of the approach has yet to come.

Even some of the most innovative work of the MDTA centers, and more recent programs such as the TAT-Oak Ridge High School partnership with Atomic Energy Commission facilities,[15] are primarily fixed-length, generalized training programs. The TAT-Oak Ridge does change to adapt to changes in demand for occupational and technical skill training through market surveys. The flexibility to change is provided by the existence of considerable plant and equipment used for production and made available as a complementarity for training as needed. A future model may, where there is a large industrial base permitting such flexibility and change in training programs, follow the TAT approach.

Where there is not such a facility the training may have to be shifted around to dispersed work sites, as in some MDTA training programs, offered through contract/project arrangements, or provided through mobile work crews who travel to work/training sites. These arrangements, shown in Figure 4-1 in the adaptation segment, may be very important for future programs in areas where there is not a heavy concentration of industry. The mobility and flexibility of the programs permits adaptation to local situations without major investment in training facilities at centers. Combinations of a center with outreach through mobile work and training arrangements is also possible, and in fact desirable, since supporting services of testing, counseling, placement, and job support are best concentrated in a central location. The Calcutta CYSEC program combines centers, dispersed sites, mobile teams, and contract/projects, but the scale of operation is small and experience with it has been limited.

Center staffs can also coordinate survey and development of job and training opportunities, since such surveys have to extend over fairly large domains in order to characterize needs within a definable labor market area. Constant surveys, rather than continuing registry statistics, are necessary in order to assess changing conditions and to avoid saturation of job markets by overproduction in certain training and skill areas. Though there is a dream of huge computerized job-demand-and-supply banks that provide instant and current information, and through some mysterious fashion auto-up-date their own files, the likelihood is that the future, as well as the present and immediate past, will be more usefully served by local information that is exact and current. Research and investment needs in data gathering and information processing for maintaining the kind of flexible arrangements for training envisaged in the adaptation segment of the future will be dealt with in a later section. Here the central concern is with training- and support-program features.

Mobile and Dispersed-Site Programs. The dispersed work-site arrangements, work crews, and contract/project possibilities can serve school-based work/study programs as well as out-of-school worker training programs. The future is likely to blur the distinctions, inasmuch as many older workers participating in retraining programs may be job based or temporarily unemployed, but also in need of general education furnished by the schools. There are various possibilities of making the contract and project service enterprises for-profit as well as nonprofit investment primarily for training.

The sustaining advantage of for-profit enterprise is obvious, even if the profits pay only a portion of the expenses. The sense of reality and the resulting motivation and the enhanced sense of worth and status provided by profit and shared earnings is also important. Most program efforts must be offered on both a profit and nonprofit basis, depending on projects and fields of training, and this has certain dangers. Some prospects are excellent in providing training that will lead to employment, but are unlikely earners or profit-makers on a project basis. Too much stress on profit, by setting up projects too explicitly as profit centers, can be harmful. It can mean not entering projects that are promising fields of training and employment because the production cum training phase is not profitable. It can also mean closing down training projects before they have satisfied job market demand. A fine balance must be maintained.

In mobile- and dispersed-site programs, the task of the work-training co-ordinator is very demanding, and here the selection of trained and experienced coordinators is important. If there are no trained or experienced prospects to fill work coordinator roles, then a training program must be developed. The requirements are quite broad, and include ability to survey product markets and job markets, deduce training-response requirements, locate job opportunities, and relate the work to training centers or institutions. They may also require entrepreneurial talent, especially if the program aims at creating small enterprises for self-employment. Self-employment programs, to be dealt with in the actualization segment, offer a return that goes beyond that provided by entry-level employment and a job.

Similar to self-employment through small industry development and training programs on dispersed sites are programs for training individuals and their families in their place of residence. The enterprise here is more often cottage or craft products, and the problem is usually not so much one of training, for the crafts may be traditional, as assistance in developing new product designs, markets, and distribution outlets, and providing the small amount of investment and working capital necessary to develop and sustain nascent enterprises. Training may be required, to renew old skills or introduce design modifications, and so the programs should be included in this section.

One difficulty that all innovative programs have, and this sometimes leads to a premature death of such enterprises, is the tendency to oversell themselves and to overpromise results, and to underestimate operating costs initially. These programs are neither easy to run nor highly cost efficient, at least in the short run. They may in the long run be effective and even cost effective, but a substantial effort and investment must be made to get them running and keep them running in their developmental stages. An even more substantial effort is needed to maintain the support and enthusiasm and cooperation of the outside sponsors who must sustain them. Shortly after the trial period and a few initial and promising results, there tends to be a flagging of energy and enthusiasm, especially by private-industry partners, as the novelty wears off, or the acute need that generated the initiative in the first place wears down. Corresponding to this phase of flagging enthusiasm by outside partners, there tends to be an escalation of rhetoric and promise by the full-time directors, trainers, and coordinators of the program staff. A lot more is said to have been accomplished than reality demonstrates.

For the future, research effort should not so much be directed at starting innovative programs as at sustaining them, especially in the critical stages, after the first enthusiasm wears off. The problem is to sustain the motivation and dedication of trainee participants, program staff, and public and private officials, after something less than complete success has rewarded their efforts. Creation of employment, and training, especially of disadvantaged groups, are not easy or quick enterprises, and failure is a constant threat. The thrust of research should be on how to accommodate to constant failure so that final success is possible. This seems a banal and obvious point, but it should be poignant for anyone who has worked in such programs.

Apprenticeship Programs. Apprenticeship programs are too well established and accepted to need much discussion as a future possibility. Past developments in the US have been reviewed in Chapter 3. Programs are more often based in a single industry or industry group in the United States, but in many developing countries they are nationally legislated programs that span all industries that employ above a certain number of workers. Under national programs, industries must either provide training on their own premises or arrange for it in centers or in other industries. Incentives are offered in the form of tax deductions or subsidies, and disincentives to ignore legislation are provided in the form of fines and penalties for violation. In many places violations are widespread and enforcement weak, and this is particularly so when the economy is sluggish and job requirements low. This weakness, added to management resistance, and sometimes union opposition, may prevent future legislated compliance with apprenticeship quotas in US industry, although there is a Bureau of Apprenticeship Training to foster and oversee programs.

Stereotypes to the contrary, educators, particularly those not directly in the vocational education field, do not have to be convinced of the merits of shifting the vocational training burden to apprenticeship and on-the-job training. In fact, many of them have great faith in the all-round effectiveness of apprenticeship and on-job training. We have not seen a general body of evidence to support total effectiveness of apprenticeship training, but the *Work in America* report attributes such statements to Mangum.[16]

Though faith in the effectiveness of apprenticeship training may be warranted by observing high quality programs such as General Electric once ran in Pittsfield or the kind that was once offered in the machine shops of New England, or the kind that Mercedes Benz runs in Europe and overseas, there are poor apprenticeship programs in the world just as there are poor vocational-school programs. Apart from quality, there is even less justification for faith in the possibility of private industry assuming the burden of vocational training through apprenticeship and on-the-job-training programs. This has not happened in the United States in single industry programs, nor has it happened in the developing countries in nationally legislated programs, despite some important contributions from SENA in Brazil, INCE in Venezuela, SENAI in Colombia, and programs in Japan and Europe. It is not likely to happen in the future in the United States.

Apprenticeship programs will go on in the United States in the years ahead, at varying levels of effectiveness and size, but the main burden of vocational training will not be assumed through this means. One problem is that the skills, once developed, are vested and movable assets, and workers can take them on to the next industry. In the future the vesting of pension plans may even increase the mobility of company-trained workers, but the tight job market may cut down on the workers' possibilities to move on to other firms.

More likely is the mix of approaches that are suggested by Figure 4-1. No one industry or group of them, however large, would take on any substantial share of the vocational-training burden that lies ahead. Apart from the fact that it is not in the interest of the industry to do so, other than filling its own specific needs, there is a huge dispersed small-industry and service requirement that could not be filled by a few large-industry programs. Nor are government-legislated apprenticeship programs the solution, especially in periods of slow employment growth. In West Bengal, one of India's most industrialized areas around Calcutta, over the past three years not one industry has hired a worker trained in its own programs.[17] Even in the steel and heavy-industry center of Jamshedpur the excellent Mercedes Benz apprenticeship program based in the Tata works produces trainees who are rarely hired by the Tata firm itself.

In the future, on-the-job training will be an important component of vocational training, whether or not it is an incorporated segment of an apprenticeship training program. With more older workers hanging on to their job base in conditions of slow employment growth, on-the-job training will often be combined with other kinds of mobile and centralized training and education offered in schools and centers. OJT will become a more effective supplement to cooperative and work/study programs in which the on-job-training component is presently very weak; in fact is largely not even noticeable.

On-the-job training runs through a range from very formal, where it may shade into the usual format of an apprenticeship program, to less formal but still observable and explicit attention to training, down to incidental training that may come as a spin-off from straight production. Incidental training may be a few words of advice or guidance from the foreman or master mechanic and a pile of wasted stock as the operator gets the hang of things. Historically, the vast amount of on-job training has been incidental or at least highly informal, and this will not be different in the future in lines of work where workers can start as operators in a simple process and gradually gain mastery over a wider scope of work. Automation may lead to some decrease in this possibility, but it may just as likely lead to an increase in need for prior skill training and an increase in the need for more general and abstract learning for service in an automated process or system. The demand for professional, technical, and clerical workers will be quite high, as the projections of the detailed section indicate, but numbers graduating from schools and training institutes to meet this demand will also be high, and the possibility is that it may even be excessive. In 1975 Massachusetts postsecondary junior colleges offering training programs directly related to professional support jobs, laboratory technicians, health specialists, and engineering associates were filled beyond capacity. Concern for high-unemployment prospects already forced a shift toward more work-related education, and rising unemployment itself increased the number of applicants who might otherwise have gone directly into the work force. Even if demand for such specialists were sizable relative to demand in the work force it is small, and supply will probably be excess.

On-the-job training has been positioned toward the actualization segment of Figure 4-1 because it will be the means of improving workers' job opportunities once they are at work, as well as fitting them for entry to work. In fact, improvement and upgrading are more likely to be the result of on-job training. This has traditionally been the case. On-the-job training will also be used for productivity training and as the training accompaniment to job restructuring and the improvement of job opportunity and work satisfaction. When and if developments reach this point, there will be a need for accompanying general and special education, either offered on the premises or work site, or supplemented in center and formal classroom programs. Just as the activity of restructuring and improving work is only in its early stages, the design of accompanying educational and training programs is also in early development. The future will bring increased activity, and the need now is for research and design and trial of experimental programs in which education and training are developed as appropriate accompaniment to job development. This is the upper end of the career-education enterprise, and there will be further treatment of this important theme.

An important section of the adaptation program segment has been skipped, i.e., programs designed for special population groups, the disadvantaged, and handicapped, some in institutionalized situations, some in open situations and some in halfway stations. Here the need is to provide special supportive services, psychological and physical, and to control working environments and the conditions of employment. In some cases the support and control can be temporary, but in some individual cases the services must be permanent. Vestibule jobs, with heavy support and control, are one form of adjustive or adaptive situation for which training, supervision, and support must be supplied. Sheltered shops, sometimes run for profit but always run with controlled conditions and special patterns of organization, offer another possibility. This may be the only lifetime working situation to which a handicapped worker can accommodate. Programs may also be based within institutions and be adapted to the special surroundings. These may be adjustment programs accompanied by off-premises work and training.

A projection of increased or decreased need for specialized programs for the handicapped or institutionalized is beyond the medical and social-science competence of this exercise. Whether there will be fewer or more physically handicapped people in the future prompts a chain of rather ghoulish speculation. Prenatal diagnosis and abortion may lead to fewer defective births, improved health care and treatment may lead to more years of survival—it does not seem useful to run further along this line of speculation.

The same is true of estimates of future prison populations on the basis of social pathology. Will more understanding and less rigorous legal treatment lead to more or less crime and imprisonment? Will there be fewer people in institutions to be served through training and work programs? Some developments are foreseeable. As social responsiveness broadens in the present and immediate future, there will be increased service, and larger numbers of handicapped and disadvantaged populations will be identified. Since there is still an unserved backlog in many areas the early part of the forecast period can only bring an increase in client populations to be reached. Also the form of address to the problem will change, and handicapped populations will increasingly be served in open situations with schooling, training, and job placement and support much like that offered to general population groups. There will be an increased need for sheltered, vestibular, and supported adaptive training and work-experience situations. Increased numbers of handicapped must be accommodated in cooperative and work/study programs, and in fact in the entire range of career-education approaches. The same is true of those disadvantaged mentally, emotionally, and socially. The trend toward deinstitutionalization seems quite strong and not likely to abate. More people will have to be served in regular school and training programs, and through adaptive training and work programs. More will be served as residents in half-way situations. Fewer inmates may be served in a completely institutionalized setting. From a standpoint of realistic working and training conditions this is all to the good.

The burden of supporting such programs may be very large. In a period of slower growth and less prosperity there may be diminished resources for such programs. With tighter employment, program adjustments may have to be maintained longer, with resulting increase in support costs. However, the provision of service itself will generate employment in the area of special education and instruction and training for the handicapped. Whether the larger resource requirements for serving special-need groups will divert funds from regular programs is also a question to ponder.

Ideally, there will be a diminished racial and ethnic cast to disadvantage, but this will not come immediately, and there will be groups of workers who are specially disadvantaged by discrimination, or by language, or early poverty and lack of educational opportunity. Indications are that racial gaps in earnings and job opportunities are closing very slowly, and there will be continuing program attention to this during the period. With current high unemployment the gap could widen again. With slowing economic growth over the longer term ahead, the problem could be exacerbated over time. Even if no ground is lost, there has been too little ground gained to permit the future to settle down at the present level. Compensatory programs to make up for language disadvantage, early and poor education, lack of familiarity with job opportunities, and education and job discrimination will take just as large a share of resources over the early period of the forecast; and will diminish over the later period only in proportion to the adequacy of the response in the earlier period. Programs must cover the entire gamut, from preparation to actualization, with special need for the latter, since many of the disadvantaged have been long stuck in mean job situations, and upgrading and enrichment of opportunity is vitally needed.

Programs for ethnic and disadvantaged groups, native Americans, migrants, and non-English-speakers appear mainly under Title III of CETA, 1973, and are directed primarily to provision of employment, training, and special supporting services. The same groups are eligible under other titles of the act, especially for the comprehensive manpower services in Title I, and public employment covered under Title II. Programmatically the main distinctions for this group will be the need for more direct assistance in securing basic employment and the need for more supportive services, before, during, and after training. There is nothing new in this. For the future the change will come mainly in the need to provide more access to more favorable career opportunities, job restructuring for those in existing employment, and retraining and development for career progress. This will be appropriate accompaniment to the opening of occupations and professions, where opportunities for access and advancement have been restricted. The rise in general educational opportunity will make larger proportions of these groups eligible.

The situation is somewhat similar for women. Projections indicate not only that larger percentages of women in all age groups will be participating in the work force, but there will also be changes in female participation in occupations once closed or restricted. The consequences of this are not so much for changed training programs as changed selection and admission procedures to the programs. The same opportunities for entrance to new careers and for retraining and upgrading of opportunities are needed.

Since employment growth projections indicate the highest growth rates and greatest job stability in the service sector and in white-collar occupations, and these have been traditionally more "open" to women (as long as they did not try to run things), then the future for women's employment opportunity is fairly promising. The years should bring an increasing equalization of job opportunities and rewards, but the consequences of this are mainly for admission and selection into job training programs rather than for change in the content and form of the program. Future openness and flexibility in program scheduling can only benefit women with home duties; provision of attached daycare support will also help; and substantial provision of retraining opportunities for older age groups will facilitate entry, exit, and re-entry to working status, with loss of skills and earnings minimized. Proposals for other accompanying legislation, e.g., to protect job tenure, is beyond the limited concern of this program review.

Youth Mobilization Programs. Youth mobilization programs, as they have developed either in the United States or in other countries, have not been limited in purpose to the training and employment of young people. As the word *mobilization* suggests, the aims go beyond employment and training to cover political and social objectives, as well as economic goals. Very often the programs are designed as a response to an emergency situation. In the United States the Civilian Conservation Corps was designed to meet the problems of the Great Depression, when massive numbers of young people were unemployed and without prospect of employment.

The CCC experience aimed to provide discipline and purpose. At the same time there were many public-works jobs in the forests and parks and waterways that needed to be done. Putting the needs of the young people and the needs of the country together in a program that would offer work, discipline, and some training seemed a natural program possibility. The general evaluation of the CCC, based on success in youth development and in the development and maintenance of natural resources, has been favorable. Similar situations exist in other countries where large numbers of young people are given work and discipline and training through national mobilization of youth. In newly developing countries the aim may also be to use the youth-corps experience to foster a sense of national identity and purpose. Training is a component of youth mobilization programs, but their purposes are by no means limited to this; they also cover work discipline, socialization, and political and civic development.

Given that most such programs are designed for young people without previous work experience, the training component of youth mobilization programs would generally be classified as prepreparation, in the sense of being prevocational. This need not be the case, and the gathering of large numbers of young people into camps and large projects provides a considerable opportunity to offer training and employment experience. This is particularly true for youths from rural and isolated regions of thin population and limited training and vocational opportunity. If demand for the program is to be influenced primarily by the numbers of young men and women in the age group relative to other age groups, the future does not indicate much need for the program.

However, the program can be justified on the basis that there are certain small but important groups that can only be served with education and training opportunities through camp or center programs. Also there is important public work to be done by groups operating from these centers. Under Title IV of CETA, Job Corps centers and Civilian Conservation centers are being established. The centers will serve rural areas with programs designed to conserve, develop, or manage public natural resources and recreation areas. The centers will also foster programs of community development. That there is a need for such work in rural areas is clear. The programs are also designed to provide training and work experience for youth from rural areas. Again this is an important justification for the program. The thin populations and scanty work-experience opportunities in such areas make it unlikely that work experience and training could be offered in any other form.

Vast numbers of youth will not have to be served, but an important segment of young people who might otherwise not have such opportunities will be provided for, and the projects will result in beneficial programs of public works and service. Present programs are small, but there is a presumption that the program size can be expanded rapidly if the situation warrants it. The current high unemployment, with the usual very high rates for young people and minority youth groups, may test this presumption immediately.

Actualization

It is in this sector that future program developments have the furthest to go, and research-and-development programs are most necessary to chart the way. Programs for preparation and adaptation, for creating entry-level jobs and preparing workers for them, and for helping workers prepare for changing job requirements at or about the same level of employment opportunity have had much more attention, support, and innovative development in the recent past. The future will not lessen the need for employment creation, entry-level training, and retraining, for these are basic to economic performance and growth in production and employment; but the indications are that programs must go considerably beyond this to fill out career development across the entire range of possibilities.

Program efforts in this area are so new, small, and dispersed that it is difficult to devise an appropriate term to cover all activities in the area. *Actualization*, the term chosen, may not be a happy choice, but *development* seems vague and general and the term is overused; *improvement* (work and worker) did not attract, and *realization* and *amelioration* are as inadequate as *actualization*. The term should be adequate to describe program activities of continuous improvement and development of work and workers. The main thrust of program activity in this segment covers:

1. Creating jobs or employment opportunities that are satisfying and rewarding in the first place, or that have the potential for providing increased advancement, reward, and satisfaction. Though primarily job creation and development, there is also an important education, training, and job-support component to this activity.

2. Redesigning and reorganizing work processes and procedures in order to restructure and improve jobs. This may also include restructuring professional performance requirements and responsibilities.

There is less of direct education and training activity here, although there will be re-education and retraining preceding the redesign, accompanying the re-organization, and in preparing managers, supervisors, and workers for the modified new performance requirements engendered by the modified process.

3. Providing continuing education and training that enables job-holders to move to different and more responsible and satisfying positions, or to create more satisfying conditions on current jobs. When these efforts are systematized and linked over time they may be part of a general career-development education. This activity is primarily education and training.

The Need for Job Development. In preceding sections the point was made that there was no one cause for job and career dissatisfaction, and that different workers demanded different returns from their work, over and above the provision of adequate earnings and working conditions. Terkel and other investigators and commentators turn up widely different reasons for the failure of jobs to satisfy job-holders, and in some cases these reasons conflict with each other and with reality. Conditions that may satisfy one worker may be a matter of indifference or a cause for alarm for another. Some workers demand a great deal of autonomy or independence, while others prefer structure and, if not outright dependence, then a high degree of support from others. Some workers may want security and some risk; some wish to see a tangible product and complete result from their labors; and others may settle for the safety of partial and anonymous contribution to a greater effort—some want the satisfaction of serving society; some care little about this. A few wish to exercise creativity. Some like to solve problems, the more unstructured the better; others need routine tasks. Many seek a sense of participation and sharing in decisions that affect them. Some want freedom from routine and restriction; others, particularly older workers, miss having a definite place to go to at a definite time. No one set of program responses to job restructuring can satisfy all the widely different demands that workers make on their jobs and means of livelihood. No program will ever satisfy all, or bring total and perpetual contentment to humankind at work; or create job and career paradises.

Those who recommend a deschooled society in the future ignore the powerful psychic return that the promise and open-endedness of schooling and student status provide. As formal schooling may never match the action and realism of the work place and the job, so the job, by the very pervasiveness of reality, never matches the promise and open-ended potential of schooling and study. The very reality of the job suggests to the worker that this is all there is; there is no more. The answer to the ills of formal schooling is not early flight to the job, for there are more unhappy work situations than school situations, and reform must go forward in both places.

There are some underlying causes of dissatisfaction running in a wide stripe through many job and work situations, and job restructuring, upgrading, and training can respond to these causes for discontent. Without program response at this end of the possibility range, career education is incomplete.

Creation and Development of New Jobs. The problem begins with not having an opportunity to explore and choose jobs that match individual expectations in the first place; and with the fact that some job and career opportunities are never open to some, even as possibilities. This problem is not answered by the fact, though indisputable, that some do not have the special aptitudes, the general intelligence, the natural talent, the physical equipment, or the determination and perseverance to seize such opportunities successfully if they had them. There is still a wide range of opportunities that are missed because of lack of foreknowledge, and circumstances unrelated to individual potential. Presumably, career education, as it is developed early in formal, general, and vocational education and as it is supplemented by guidance, counseling, and support, will respond to the problem of opportunities missed through lack of knowledge of their existence. But knowing about the opportunities is insufficient if career jobs are still inaccessible to people even after they learn about them. In fact, this frustration will increase discontent and lack of fit between worker and whatever work he does get. There must be programs to create job opportunities and to train and assist people to get them. A few such programs are listed to begin the actualization segment.

Development of Self-Employment. Training and support for the development of small enterprises for self-employment is one such possibility, and it receives fairly meager attention and support in US policy and program approaches. This type of opportunity is aimed at those who wish independence and autonomy, and are willing to assume risk, or tolerate the lack of security that comes without dependence on another for the provision of an assured paycheck.

There are a variety of government-aided programs for assisting creation, maintenance, and growth of small enterprises, and assistance for these enterprises is also a regularly established feature of commercial banks and private agencies. Special programs have been developed and run by government, foundation, and community-development agencies to stimulate and support entrepreneurial activity among disadvantaged groups. Community-development corporations support such programs. As an outcome of some MDTA and OEO training programs, graduates have started small production, service, and sales enterprises. Still there have been few large and systematic attempts to join training and small-business support into a comprehensive program for small industry and self-employment.

These programs require assistance in identifying and developing markets for products or services, assistance in training for producing the goods or providing the services, provision of credit, business management support, and for some, strong counseling and supportive services over a period of time. The programs may also require assistance in the form of concessional licensing, access to land, plant, or sales space, and cooperative marketing.

Programs, though still small and scattered, are beginning to spread in developing countries, where the possibility of employment in large, modern sector enterprises is small and slow to grow. The example of one of them, Calcutta Youth Self-Employment Center, has been mentioned. The advantages of small-enterprise and self-employment programs, though costly and difficult to develop and run, are that they create employment, stimulate economic activity, and provide more satisfying opportunities for those who seek independence and autonomy. The disadvantage, in a highly developed economy and technology such as the US, is that small-enterprise development seems counter to the trend of enlarging and agglomerating enterprises which may destroy or marginalize small, single-purpose enterprises.

There is no clear trend in the forecasts of the US economy and the employment status of the work force to indicate that there will be increased opportunity for independent enterprise and self-employment in the future. In fact, some trends that have been running indicate the opposite. Forecasts of the future do not stress this kind of opportunity, but there are some signs and countertrends that indicate that change is possible, and that program support should be forthcoming to support such changes. Trends in franchising many small and independent outlets, rather than direct centralized management of them, is one sign. The rise of small shops and craft outlets is another. The large numbers of opportunities in professional- and technical-level services that now exist will increase. Forecasts indicate high growth potential here. As job openings in large and organized enterprises slow, there will be more people ready, if not prepared, to venture into independent efforts. It is also true that in very hard times, as in the present depression, more small enterprises fail. Apart from the merits of such future enterprises on purely economic and technical terms, there is the return provided for those in overly structured and organized situations who seek independence and are willing to pay the price of diminished security.

Development of New Jobs and Careers in Large Public and Private Organizations. Activity in this area has mainly been aimed at the provision of new, modified, or increased public and community services, although there are opportunities for development of such new jobs and services in private industry. The rise of environmental concern has produced new opportunities for public and private employment, and HEW has made program response to this need by encouraging new training programs for new fields, especially in postsecondary technical institutions. An additional feature has been the attempt to open these new opportunities to disadvantaged and minority groups.

Efforts are inadequate currently. The Public Services Careers program has actually shown declining coverage, from 66 thousand in 1972 to less than 25 thousand in 1973, and under CETA it is not clear what the type and level of activity will be. Public service employment is provided for under CETA Title II, but it is not clear how much career development or opportunity the programs will offer. Currently, expansion of these programs is under way, and the difficulty of expanding the programs sensibly and with equity in the height of a depressed economic situation is already apparent. The object of the present programs is simply to furnish jobs to the unemployed, and development of career opportunities and job enrichment seems farfetched in the present difficult times.

The New Careers Program is covered under special responsibility programs in Title III, but again there is a question both of the significance and the size and the aim of the program. Recently there has been great stress on the need to train people for new careers in health services, but already there are strong signs of overproduction and resultant unemployment in these fields in New York.[18] The decline in job opportunities in education has followed the decline in enrollments that began in the late sixties and is still running its course except in a few special geographical areas and fields. Under the "other programs" category in a report on federally assisted work and training programs for 1972-74 there were assorted programs for training for social services and rehabilitation,[19] but most of these programs were never large and now appear to be in decline, indicating that however needed the services may be, without public funds to sustain them, the programs wither and die.

Yet the future indicates that there will be a need for expanding programs that train for new careers and opportunities in public services. First, the client need of the recipients of the service is there, and most such programs can increase markedly without saturation of the field of need. Secondly, there will be a need to stimulate jobs and job-opportunity development through public support of such programs. Some programs will have a career opportunity and development component, some will simply be providing entry-level jobs and some income maintenance at a subsistence level, as in the work-incentive programs.

Opportunities in education will increase all through 1980-90, beginning with an upturn in primary-school enrollments after 1980. In absolute terms enrollments will not rise to the levels of the peak years of the middle fifties in primary schools and the middle sixties in secondary schools. The rise in enrollment forecast for the early 1980s simply means a rise relative to enrollments in the years immediately preceding. In secondary schools enrollments will be increasing from the late 1980s through the end of the century. The potential for providing satisfactory employment in teaching is very large, for the pupil/teacher ratios that have prevailed over the past period of rapid expansion are products of necessity, convention, and dubious economy.

In the years ahead it is likely that pupil/teacher ratios will lower as enrollments decline, but tenure and union agreements prevent proportionate reduction in staff. It will be interesting to observe whether or not these ratios will be maintained as enrollment edges up again. If so, employment gain in these fields can be large, and programs to provide against this contingency should be planned. Teaching will provide not only entry jobs but job-development possibilities through continuing education and training in-service. Slow economic growth and slow growth in available revenues may hold the opportunity down, but slow growth in employment opportunities for educated people may force them up. Replacement of older teachers will also make jobs.

The possibility of fostering new job opportunities in large private enterprises is not likely to be any more promising in the future than it has been in the past. Some new matters of public concerns backed up by enforcement, e.g., environmental concern and antipollution, may generate some new occupations with career promise, but more likely these will be filled by trained professionals and technical people already in the employ of the firm, and the numbers and opportunities will not be large in any case. Such activity in private enterprise situations will more appropriately come under the next section, Job Redesign and Restructuring.

Job Development Through the Restructuring of Work and Occupational Requirements. This topic requires greater attention and a more adequate development than this chapter permits, and more specialized knowledge than the writers possess; but the theme must be touched upon, however briefly, in any rounded treatment of career education and work-related training program possibilities. Job restructuring to provide greater satisfaction and self-actualization for workers is an important topic for the future, and it has important implications for the development of education and training programs. The Special Task Force Report, *Work in America*, makes a strong case for the need to restructure and "humanize" jobs, in order to provide increased satisfaction to workers with increasing levels of educational attainment.[20] This seems an inadequate justification, for the numbers of college and university graduates may not grow as in the past, and the relationship between satisfaction and educational attainment level is not clearly established. Still the main thesis is justified if reported dissatisfaction of workers with all levels of education is to be credited.

The alarming reports on absenteeism, plant, equipment, stock, and product damage, lowered productivity, and manifest dissatisfaction with the present form of work organization provide indication of need. *Work in America* also described in outline form more than thirty pilot programs for the redesign of work in US and in European-managed plants. The same report outlines a program for basic worker self-renewal which aims to take workers from slow growth industry and skill areas and retrain them for placement in faster growth occupations and industries. Though there is a self-improvement component to this program suggestion, the major purpose seems to be adaptation. Workers would be trained to move up the skill ladder, thus vacating opportunities at lower levels for new entrants and unskilled workers. In this section the main concern is not changing workers to fit jobs so much as changing jobs to fit workers.

Job-restructuring efforts aim at responding to some of the causes for dissatisfaction that have been mentioned. Greater participation is allowed in designing production and assembly processes and in job and work scheduling. Workers are given a voice in decisions and increased control over their work lives. Supervision is made less constant and intrusive. Scheduling is less rigid, work hours more flexible, and more responsibility for attaining required output targets is left to workers. In some cases there is greater sharing of information on goals and costs and profits, concerns once reserved to a few in higher management. Workers are allowed to participate in various stages of production and assembly so that a tangible result of their efforts is observable. Work is redesigned to provide more sense of participation, more sense of completion and fulfillment, more sense of efficacy and self-direction, more freedom to adjust work schedules to individual needs, more autonomy, more social interaction, more information on general goals, and increased understanding of the rationale for policies and regulations.

Career education and work-directed education and training programs can respond to the need for job and work restructuring and the enrichment of employment opportunities in various ways:

1. By informing future workers of the possibility for participation in job restructuring and work enrichment.

2. By helping future workers identify and articulate their own needs and work-satisfaction requirements, and helping to improve the fit between future workers and their requirements.

3. By enhancing cooperation between workers and managers. Inasmuch as schools train managers and employers as well as workers the same information and guidance services should be available to both groups, thus enhancing the likelihood of cooperation.

4. By training managers, supervisors, and workers for the changed work requirements engendered by restructuring and enrichment efforts. Here, career education at its upper limits will have a substantial future contribution to make.

Providing Continuing Education and Training. The enrichment of work opportunities by the creation of new and more satisfying jobs, the restructuring and improvement of existing ones, and the provision of continuing education and training to help people advance and improve their job and career opportunities are the major program objectives at the more advanced levels of career education. It is at this point that education and training programs shift from training for jobs and employment and informing people about careers, to education and training explicitly designed for career development. There are these main aspects of such programs:

1. Some training will be directly related to the process of restructuring work and jobs. It will be incorporated into the process itself and cover the design of the restructuring efforts and the changes necessary in manager, supervisor, and worker performance for adaptation to changed work requirements. These programs go beyond conventional training for productivity or leadership, to training for increased participation in the change process itself. This is the field of organizational behavior and training specialists.

2. The changes introduced in redesigned and restructured work situations will introduce new requirements which in turn will change professions and occupations. Training programs must respond to this change, and this is appropriately a part of career education program development.

3. The entire dynamic of occupations and careers may change, and this is a future charge on continuing education programs aimed at career development.

Beyond these points there is uncharted territory where programs must be developed for the preparation of workers for retirement, leisure, combinations of work and leisure, and death. Program research and development for the career education of the future must be concentrated in the earlier program categories of the actualization segment, but before the end of the forecast period there will be substantial exploration of life stages and career requirements that lie beyond these bounds.

5

Planning, Resource Allocation, and Program Delivery: the Legislative Base

Introduction

It is beyond the range of this review to attempt an analysis of the bewildering complex of law and regulation that govern the planning, resource allocation, and delivery of programs in employment-directed education. Much less is it possible to deal with the federal, state, and local, public and private administrative structures that control the operational machinery for program delivery. Still, for completeness, a final and brief section is added in order to lend some reality to the projection of future program needs and program response possibilities.

Present Legislative Base

The complexity of legislation for work-related education is evident in several areas: the number and variety of laws covering work-related education programs; the variety of target populations (client groups) served under the legislation; the variety of program types, as already discussed in Chapter 4; and the number and type of federal agencies involved. This still stops short of taking into account the maze of state and local agencies involved in delivery, and the organizations, AVA for example, that influence everything from basic legislation to program content. Beyond this lie the jungles of special public and private political and economic interests, all contributing drops of oil, or grains of sand, to the policy and administrative machinery.

Target populations to be served by federal legislation are varied. Disadvantaged youth, veterans, school-age youth, minorities, employable welfare recipients, adults with less than twelve years of education, the handicapped, American Indians, inmates, the unemployed, migrant workers, school dropouts, and the poor—to name but a few—are all recipients designated for aid under the law. Partly because of the rich variation in target populations, legislation to serve these populations takes on its own variety.

As diverse target groups with diverse needs were identified as clients to be served, a varied federal legislative response was prompted. The Manpower Information Service lists no fewer than twenty-one different laws that formed the authorizing legislation for federally assisted manpower programs in 1974 (see Appendix A). These laws provide the basis for numerous programs, running the gamut from career education, preemployment services, on-the-job training for entry level positions, and other programs shown in detail in Chapter 4. The list

119

in Appendix A, though recent, is not complete or current, for new legislation has appeared or is in the process of appearing. For example, congressional oversight hearings have recently gone forward on a vocational education bill that will extend or revise the Vocational Education amendments of 1968.

The current major legislative base for employment-directed education is in CETA and in the Vocational Education amendments of 1968. A summary analysis of these legislative bases will be offered, but it may be appropriate to note that even in states where vocational education and manpower development are handled by very competent and sophisticated officials, no one person claims to be a master of even the existing legislation.

In FY 1974 no fewer than eight federal departments were involved in the administration of federally assisted manpower programs. These include major participants like HEW and Labor, but also the departments of Defense, Housing and Urban Development, Interior, Justice, Transportation, and the Treasury. In addition to these, the Civil Service Commission, the Office of Economic Opportunity, and the Veterans Administration were involved in administering programs in 1974. Within the major administrators of work-related education programs there is also a diversification of administrative powers. For example, in HEW, the Division of Vocational and Technical Education, the National Institute of Education, the National Institutes of Health (Division of Allied Health Manpower and Office of Health Manpower Opportunity), the Community Services Administration, and Social and Rehabilitation Service all administer programs dealing with work and education. In the Department of Labor, the US Employment Service and the Manpower Administration (Bureau of Apprenticeship and Training, Office of National Projects, Office of Manpower Development Programs, and Regional Manpower Administrations) handle programs in our main area of interest.

The large majority of programs are administered by a single agency, but in a few cases programs are administered with the cooperation of several federal agencies. For example, Project Transition is administered by the Department of Defense with the Department of Labor and the Office of Education. Likewise the institutional training under the now repealed MDTA was administered jointly by the Department of Labor and HEW. The Work Incentive Program (WIN) also involves some joint cooperation by these same two agencies.

Some of the agencies merely disburse funds; some control through policy and regulation; some plan; and some implement programs. The complexity and diversity of laws, agencies, and programs, and the resulting duplication, jurisdictional squabbling, and omissions inevitable in such a divided world, suggest the need for consolidation, and at the very least, coordination.

Consolidation of Legislation, Organization, and Planning

Recently there has been a move toward the consolidation of some of the federally assisted programs under a single piece of legislation. The Comprehensive Employment and Training Act which was passed in December 1973, and which became effective for many programs in July 1974, has consolidated programs under the Manpower Development and Training Act and Parts A, B, and E of Title I of the Economic Opportunity Act. Basically, however, this legislation is aimed at the decategorization and decentralization of manpower and public employment programs under MDTA, while keeping categorical funding for the Job Corps and for special target groups like migrants or American Indians. It seems certain that because of the diversity of the target populations and their needs, and because of the diversity of the services provided and the specialty of services provided by the various agencies, there will remain considerable legislation to be administered.

In addition to attempts to consolidate legislation, there have been attempts to consolidate organizational responsibility at the federal level and to consolidate planning and resource allocation at the local or operational level. Discussion of a superagency for human resource development, covering manpower and education, is currently muted, but the notion was extensively discussed in recent times. The idea was also discussed in many other countries, but even in those countries where there is national, centralized, and fairly authoritative planning, creation of Human Resource Development Ministries have been difficult to accomplish. Ministries of education have generally been too powerful to assimilate with ministries of labor; and national apprenticeship programs have generally been too autonomous. There may be, however, more coherence developed through national manpower planning efforts, but even this has not brought harmony. Intensification of efforts to encourage cooperation is about the best that can be done.

Attempts to consolidate planning and resource allocation at the operating level, as in Cooperative Area Manpower Planning System (CAMPS), suggest that comprehensive and consolidated efforts will not come easily through voluntary association. Looking toward the future we see no indications that consolidation will gain ground, either in legislation, organization, or operation. CETA, as we read it, does not seem to be heading in this direction, although local councils may encourage cooperation at the operating level. One important form of cooperation is through interagency committees and task forces at federal level.

There is a view that, given client group and program complexity, lack of consolidation is all to the good. If consolidation merely implies aggregation to large size and centralization of control, this may indeed be a reasonable view, but it is less persuasive when applied to the lack of comprehensive perspective and policy and planning coherence that now prevails. Perhaps our own failure to get a comprehensive grasp of the legislative, planning, and implementation structure have led to pessimistic forecasts about future improvements in overall coherence.

Major Existing Legislation:
Comparison of Planning Structures

The major legislative base for employment-directed education is found in the Comprehensive Employment and Training Act of 1973 and the Vocational

Education amendments of 1968, now in the process of change. A brief summary of these pieces of legislation is provided in Appendix B.

Under CETA a considerable planning activity is required by Prime Sponsor Manpower Planning Councils and State Manpower Service Councils. Representatives of vocational education in the states must participate in the planning activities as members of these councils, and must also submit plans under VEA provisions. The requirements for such plans are comprehensive and extraordinarily detailed. For example, the Comprehensive Manpower Plan must offer a narrative description of program which contains a policy statement of the purpose of the program, a description of economic conditions, a description of labor-force characteristics, an assessment of skill shortages, a definition of manpower needs, a statement of general and priority groups to be served, and a statement of goals to be accomplished.

Planning demand is heavy both on the technical skills of most councils and most state staffs, and on the information base available in most situations. The requirements mentioned are only the "basics"; the planners also have to go on to relate planned results to needs in which, among other things, they must infer "how training and services will provide participants with economic self-sufficiency"[1] and "how training will lead to employment and *enhance career development.*"[2] Even the "basic" requirements seem excessively demanding. This judgment is reinforced if one compares the present level of manpower analysis in most states, the reality as it were, with the requirements of the law.

For some prime sponsor areas there may be a useful description of economic conditions available. It may not cover exactly the same territorial or labor-market domain, but it may be possible to infer something useful from larger economic and market areas. It will not be easy. Our concern will be limited to the description of the labor force characteristics, assessment of skill shortages, and definition of manpower needs and groups to be served. At the level of disaggregation, detail, and precision necessary for relating labor demand to training-program needs, the provision of such information in timely fashion for planning programs annually seems almost impossible. If the information is provided at a high level of aggregation and generality, it is difficult to see how it will serve to guide program development.

There are visions of computer-based systems spewing out such information when called up, but this is the stuff of dreams. The problem does not lie with classifying, storing, and accessing the information; the problem comes with gathering and updating in a situation of constant flux and change. While the New York City employment offices are stating that there is overcrowding and unemployment in health services, art and advertising, computer programming, construction trades, brokerages, and banking, the experts are still touting these as growth potentials for the area. Meanwhile, proprietary schools that the shrewdest of commentators like Rogers[3] see as offering great flexibility and market response are pushing these same lines as good job-training prospects through TV, and in ads in the same papers that are announcing the dismal employment prospects. Any information that prime sponsor planning councils have on assessments of skill shortages, description of labor force characteristics, and definition of manpower needs (which incidentally seems to include both the others) is likely to be several months out of date, and by the time the plan is made, the funding secured, and the training program mounted, the need is gone or changed.

Cluster analysis, and the training-program possibilities derived from the analysis, will cut down on rigidity and training response failure to some extent, but this line of development provides no general answer, especially to new entrants. Apart from the fuzziness of much of the analysis, where the analysis *is* sound it largely reflects the fact that workers already in the work force can make the same switches to allied fields when employment slows. Within firms and with union protection this is much more likely to happen. But beyond this, the problem may be that the entire field underlying some clusters has changed, and there is an oversupply of trained workers for any of the related jobs.

Nor will computerized job banks handle the problem. If job opportunities can be said to be bankable they are in banks on which there is a constant run. The whole notion of job banks and skill matches seems somewhat oversold, although again it will help avoid some of the worst misfit problems. Like many responses to employment, when overexpanded it largely solves the employment problem of those involved in solving the problem. This is no mean contribution, as the antipoverty programs demonstrated.

In addition to gains through improved job analysis and training match, and computerized job and skill demand and supply information bases, research-and-development efforts also should be examining the limits that such assistance can provide for manpower planning and the development of training programs. Instead of vast banks of detailed information, more general indicators of change that can be related to shifts in job demand may provide quicker and more useful information. Better ways of identifying sources of information, gaining the continuing cooperation of these sources, and methods for rapid and accurate assemblage and quick scanning of the general tendencies and trends of such information are needed. There should be much more effort given to developing good information sources. Analysis methods should focus on linkages between one occupation and another, between one activity and another, and between one activity and a set of occupations. These relationships should be scanned for signs, however general. The main recommendation here is that development work should go toward simplification as well as the handling of more and more detail.

On the supply or training side the direction for research and development is toward increased program flexibility, using some of the program-response possibilities examined in Chapter 4, and in some cases settling for piecewise and short-interval, special-purpose training rather than attempting training for general mastery. Perhaps the most important effort should be directed at spreading the notion that manpower planning will never see the day when information is sufficient in quantity and form to take the uncertainty out of manpower-development planning. This may save the sanity of many good men and free them for the small and adjustive tasks that keep the daily work moving forward at a reasonable pace and in a reasonable way.

The problem is that people have been quite content to move in this spasmodic way, and planners have made a contribution when they attempted to foster the notion that clearer definition of objectives and better information on program needs and responses would help. This is a good thing, but there can be too much of such a thing.

Several writers, Burkett among them,[4] have commented on the fact that most state vocational-education plans are nothing more than compliance documents that group programs according to funding and legislative categories. Our experience, which is limited to only three such state planning efforts, supports this view. One difficulty is the lack of good manpower-demand information with which to shape program directions. A more fundamental problem is that many state agencies have no one who knows how to take even the most rudimentary step in planning, establishing goals, and distinguishing goals from activities. Most so-called goal statements are nothing more than lists of activities with numbers attached. Without goals and program objectives no evaluation or assessment of past program activity is possible, and no setting of future program objectives is likely. Hence, progress or lack of it cannot be assessed. The activities become the end in themselves, i.e. the provision of forty guidance counsellors (why?), the equipping of twenty machine shops (with the program never described), enrollment of 4000 general-course students in cooperative programs (why this group, why this number, why these programs, what kind of cooperative programs?). Appendix C gives an example of a first pass at trying to develop a set of goals and objectives out of a vast welter of activities scattered through a so-called state plan.

Programs, as described in most state plans, would be difficult to assess for cost effectiveness, even if goals and objectives were specified, inasmuch as costs and budgetary requirements are detached from the program descriptions in the first place. Any competent planner could rip through most state plans, listing weaknesses of the most rudimentary sort. Rather than cataloguing them, it is perhaps better to come to a simple conclusion: a vast effort for in-service training of vocational-education planners and programmers is badly needed. Apart from a few private consultant groups helping states improve their planning, there is little technical assistance available; but legislation calls for a very large planning effort. If planning assistance and training cannot be provided, then requirements should be modified in the direction of realistic expectations, but someday the planning problem must be faced. Perhaps such help can be provided through a national program of technical assistance such as AMIDS (Area Manpower Institutes for the Development of Staff), which provided assistance to MDTA administrators.

Appendixes

Appendix A: Legislation Covering Federally Assisted Manpower Programs, Fiscal Year 1974

National Defense Act of 1916
Manpower Development and Training Act
Adult Basic Education Act of 1966
Vocational Education Act of 1963
Vocational Education Amendments of 1968
Education Amendments of 1972
Allied Health Professions Personnel Training Act of 1966
Health Manpower Training Act of 1970
Social Security Act
Comprehensive Health Manpower Training Act of 1971
Vocational Rehabilitation Act of 1920 as amended
Housing Act of 1964
Demonstration Cities and Metropolitan Development Act, 1966
Indian Adult Vocational Training Act of 1958
Youth Conservation Act of 1970
National Apprenticeship Act of 1937 (Fitzgerald Act)
Economic Opportunity Act of 1964
Wagner-Peyser Act of 1933
Emergency Employment Act of 1971
Federal Aid Highway Act of 1971
Revenue Act of 1971
Veterans' Readjustment Benefits Act of 1936, as amended

Source: "Guide to Federally Assisted Manpower Programs," *Manpower Information Service*, p. 21:1004.

Other pertinent laws include the following:

Public Health Service Act, as amended
Nurse Training Act of 1971
Veterans' Vocational Rehabilitation Benefits Act, as amended
Veterans' Education and Training Amendments Act of 1970
Public Works and Economic Development Act of 1965
Elementary and Secondary Education Act of 1965, as amended
Older Americans' Act in 1965, as amended
Comprehensive Employment and Training Act

Appendix B:
A Summary of Major
Legislation for
Work-Related
Education

Comprehensive Employment and Training Act (CETA), 1973[a]

1. General Introduction

   a. Legislative Titles:

   Title I: Comprehensive Manpower Services; Title II: Public Employment Programs; Title III: Special Federal Responsibilities; Title IV: Job Corps; Title V.: National Commission for Manpower Policy; Title VI: General Provisions

   Both Title I and Title II provide funds that are available for the full range of manpower programs, the distinction between titles being in the distribution formulas by which funds are allocated.

   b. Decategorization and Decentralization of Manpower Programs

   The Secretary of Labor, under CETA provisions, now makes block grants to more than 400 local and state governments to plan and operate manpower programs. Funds are channeled to the communities through these prime sponsors. This is a move toward both the decategorization and decentralization of manpower programs.

2. Funding

   a. Distribution Formulas

   Title I: 80% of the funds available are apportioned among states and areas within states according to:

   50% of the funds in accordance with the ratio that the manpower funds received by the area in the previous year bear to the total manpower funds distributed under this title;

---

[a]Much of the summary of CETA legislation is based upon the good discussion provided by Robert Guttman, "Intergovernmental Relations Under the New Manpower Act," pp. 10-16.

37.5% are distributed in accordance with the ratio that the number of unemployed in the area bears to the total unemployed;

12.5% are distributed in accordance with the ratio that the number of adults in families with annual incomes below $7000 bears to all such adults.

20% of the funds are available to the Secretary of Labor to be distrubuted thusly:

5% are available only for special grants for vocational education;

1% are available to staff manpower planning councils;

4% are available for state provided manpower services;

5% are available to promote voluntary combinations of prime sponsors to form consortia.

The remaining 5% is used at the Secretary's discretion to bring all areas up to 90% of last year's funding level and to continue funding of programs of demonstrated effectiveness.

Title II: Prime sponsors (or an Indian tribe on a state or federal reservation) qualify for assistance if they represent an area of substantial unemployment, i.e., an unemployment rate of 6.5% or more for three consecutive months. The distribution formula is according to:

80% of the funds are distributed in the ratio that the number of unemployed in the area bears to the total number unemployed in all eligible areas;

20% of the funds are discretionary funds to be distributed by the Secretary of Labor after taking into account the unemployment in the area.

Title III: The Secretary of Labor is given responsibility for certain groups:

(i) Special manpower target groups: youth, older people, offenders, non-English-speakers, etc.;

(ii) American Indians: funds equal to 3.2% of Title I funds are available;

(iii) Migrant and seasonal workers: funds equal to 4% of Title I funds are available;

(iv) Urban and rural areas with large concentrations of low-income, unemployed, or rural areas with substantial outmigration;

(v) Technical assistance, labor market information job bank, evaluation, research, and development.

Title IV: General Funding of Job Corps

b. Timing of Funding

To afford adequate notice of funding available under CETA, the act provides that appropriations can be included in an appropriation act for the fiscal year preceding the fiscal year for which they are available for obligation. There is general uncertainty whether this will actually happen, or whether it will go along on a yearly basis.

3. Planning

a. Role of State and Local Government

The law carefully specifies the administrative roles of federal, state, and local governments and local interest groups in providing manpower services. This is contained in the definition of a prime sponsor for manpower programs and also in provisions defining the relationship of the local prime sponsor to the State.

CETA defines a local prime sponsor as any unit of general local government—city or county—with a population of 100,000 or more. The state governments act as the prime sponsors for areas that do not meet the minimum population criterion. This definition of prime sponsor means that approximately 2/3 of the population will be in areas with city and county prime sponsors, and 1/3 of the population will have the state governments as the prime sponsor. There is also the provision of incentives for units of local government to combine to form a prime sponsor consortium, although one of the existing partner units must meet the required population size. This provision has already stimulated a substantial effort to form consortiums.

Other provisions that define the relation of the local prime sponsor to the state include:

(i) The local prime sponsor may use state services to whatever extent the local prime sponsor finds appropriate. *For example, there is no federal requirement on the use of the Employment Service or the vocational educational system by the prime sponsors.*

(ii) The state is required to cooperate in implementing the local plan.

(iii) There are incentives in the act to encourage local prime sponsors to use state services. There are two special funding mechanisms to promote cooperation: 5% of Title I funds are available only for vocational education to be provided after agreement between the State Board for Vocational Education and the prime sponsor, and 4% of Title I funds are available for the state to provide manpower services such as vocational education or employment services in areas served by local prime sponsors. As Guttman states, the states were given "influence rather than power."[1]

b. Role of Local Organizations

Local organizations are represented on local planning councils, which the prime sponsors appoint and staff. The councils recommend plans and procedures and monitor and evaluate local manpower programs. The client community, local organizations, the employment service, education and training agencies, and local businesses and labor groups are represented on these councils. Community action agencies and the state employment service are now simply two kinds of organizations that may conduct manpower programs.

c. Federal Role

(i) There is no requirement for the states to match federal funds.

(ii) Prime sponsors must prepare comprehensive plans for providing manpower services, and the federal government must approve the plan before a prime sponsor is funded.

(iii) The federal government also acts in the supervisory role of a monitor to ensure that performance complies with the plan and the statutory requirements. Government supervision does not extend to the details of program design—only to the broad objectives.

(iv) The federal government is also responsible for providing manpower services to target groups such as American Indians, maintaining Job Corps programs, and establishing a National Commission for Manpower Policy.

d. Planning Process

For Title I funds the planning process is relatively simple. Prime sponsors, with advice from the Manpower Planning Council, prepares a Comprehensive Manpower Plan. If the prime sponsor is a state, it must establish—in addition to a Planning Council—a State Manpower Services Council. Its function is also advisory. It is required to review and monitor all manpower activities within the state, including those of prime sponsors, and advise and make recommendations concerning manpower activities to the governor, prime sponsors, state manpower agencies, and the public. All prime sponsor plans must receive approval of the Department of Labor's assistant regional director for manpower for whatever region the prime sponsor is included within. Summaries of Title II program plans are also included in the Comprehensive Manpower Plan that each prime sponsor submits to the Department of Labor.

Vocational Education Amendments of 1968

1. General Introduction

a. Legislative Titles:

There are three titles to the amendments:

Title I—amendments to the Vocational Education Act of 1963;

Title II—Vocational Education Leadership and Professional Development Amendment of Higher Education Act of 1965; and

Title III—Miscellaneous Provisions

Title I is of main concern. It contains Parts A through I, and all of these deal with vocational education. Part B (State Vocational Education Programs) and Part C (Research and Training in Vocational Education) are funded under one authorization. Each of the parts D through I is funded separately. These parts deal with exemplary programs, residential vocational schools, consumer and homemaking education, cooperative vocational-education programs, work/study programs, and curriculum development. Part B is discussed in the rest of this summary. It is offered as an illustration of the amendments and the planning and resource allocation involved. It is relatively typical of the other parts and has by far the largest authorization.

2. Funding

a. Distribution

From funds appropriated for Part B, the Commissioner of Education is authorized to do two things:

(i) He may reserve up to $5 million per fiscal year for transfer to the Secretary of Labor to finance national, regional, state, and local studies and projections of manpower needs.

(ii) The remainder of the sum is allotted among the states on the basis of the number of persons in the various age groups needing vocational education and the per capita income in the respective states.

b. Payment to States

The Commissioner pays to the states, from the amount available to the state for grants, an amount equal to 50% of the state and local expenditures in carrying out its state plan.

c. Timing of Funding

Funding is one year at a time, which affords no advance notice. The national budget request is made early in the calendar year. States prepare their plans on the assumption that funding will remain at the same level as in the preceding year. The plans are to take effect with the beginning of the fiscal year. Appropriation bills are not usually passed until later in the calendar year, so states receive federal money under continuing resolutions passed by Congress. If the final appropriations bill contains funding at levels different than in the preceding year, then adjustments are made in payments to states. Final funding depends on approval of the state plan for vocational education and a matching of the Federal money with the state and local money.

3. Planning

a. National Advisory Council on Vocational Education

A national council was established to advise the Commissioner concerning vocational-education programs supported under the amendments, review the administration and operation of vocational-education programs under the title, and conduct independent evaluations of vocational-education programs funded under the title.

b. State Advisory Councils

Any state that desires funding under the bill must establish a State Advisory Council that advises the state board responsible for vocational education on the development and policy matters arising in the administration of the state plan; evaluates vocational-education programs, services, and activities assisted under the title; and prepares and submits through the state board to the commissioner and to the National Council an evaluation report of vocational education programs, services, and activities assisted under the title.

c. State Plans

The state must submit a state plan for approval by the Commissioner. The plan must have been prepared in consultation with the State Advisory Council and must set forth a long-range program plan, an annual program plan, the policies and procedures to be followed by the state in the distribution of funds to local education agencies; provide minimum qualifications for teachers, supervisors, and other personnel having responsibilities for vocational education in the state; provide for entering into cooperative arrangements with the system of public employment offices in the state; and set forth fiscal-control and fund-accounting procedures. In addition, the annual program plan, submitted as only a part of the state plan, must include the content and allocation of federal and state vocational education funds to programs, services, and activities.

Appendix C:
Development of a Set
of Goals and Objectives
From a State Vocational
Plan

General Goal Statement: *To expand and improve occupational education in order to increase the size and productivity of the work force*

(Statement implies a quantitative and qualitative proximate goal and a quantitative and qualitative ultimate goal. The proximate goals are supported by appropriate activities in the form of programs and inputs.)

I. Proximate Goals—Quantitative: General Client Population

   a. General Statement: To expand regular occupational education programs (increase by 75% . . .)

   (i) Increase by 7200 the number of students served by occupational education

      (a) Increase enrollment in occupational education by 2% (as a result of improved data)

   (ii) Improved retention—reduce by 30% the number of students, who, once entered in a program of occupational education do not continue their education or remain unemployed, or are underemployed.

   b. General statement: To expand occupational competence programs for students of general curriculum

   (i) Enroll 15,000 general curriculum students from 45 public secondary schools.

   (ii) Plan a statewide occupational program that will in FY 76 provide for 20,000 or 5% of the 400,000 students in the general curriculum.

   (iii) By 1980 provide for 240,000 or 60% of the 450,000 students in the general curriculum.

   c. General Statement: Expand career exploration programs for children in grades 1-9.

139

(i) Increase by 25% of the total enrollment in grades 1-9, or 30,000 the number of students exposed to career exploration and career awareness programs.

d. General Statement: Expand the number of apprenticeship opportunities in occupational programs.

(i) Expand the number of apprenticeship opportunities in occupational programs by 15%.

e. General Statement: Expand opportunities for participation in cooperative and work experience programs.

(i) Increase by 20% above FY 74 the number of businesses and industries providing cooperative learning opportunities in the Commonwealth.

(ii) Increase by 50% above FY 74 the number of occupational programs that provide students cooperative or out-of-class work experience.

II. Proximate Goals—Quantitative: Special Client Population

a. General Statement: Increase the participation of priority populations in occupational education programs.

(i) To enroll 2,000 handicapped students. (These students will come from the general curriculum and 1,000 students not currently enrolled in any state educational program.)

(ii) Expand 40% over FY 74 the enrollment in occupation education programs of minorities (7,300 students), which will:

   (a) increase black enrollment by 3000
   (b) increase enrollment of those with Spanish surnames by 2500
   (c) increase enrollment of Chinese by 1000

These enrollments will come from both the general curriculum, unemployed and underemployed dropout populations, or other individuals who lack the basic skills necessary for participation in current programs.

(iii) Increase the enrollment of women to at least 25% of the FY 74 total enrollment in occupational education programs (i.e., by 5000). (These enrollments will come particularly from those areas where there was little or no previous opportunity to participate.)

III. Proximate Goals–Qualitative: General Client Population

    a. General Statement: Improve general occupational-education programs.

        (i) Provide comprehensive curricula that relate educational offerings and skill training to both career aspirations of students and employment opportunities.

        (ii) Develop 83 new instructional programs to meet the demands for new and emerging technological occupations (in order to increase post-occupational placement by 3%, cf., III, c, [iii]).

        (iii) (Increase by 75% occupational education programs) utilizing behavioral objectives derived from analysis of specific competencies required in 100 selected occupations.

        (iv) (Improve management, planning and communication in the delivery of technical services) in order to enhance the quality of occupational education and to foster professional cooperation throughout the Commonwealth.

            (a) (Increase above FY 74, funds to expand in FY 75 the planning capability and the regionalization of management activities) for the development of occupational education.

        (v) (Foster cooperation among various state departments and agencies in the Commonwealth and encourage interstate cooperation) in order to provide for more effective occupational education programs that meet the needs of students and manpower requirements.

    b. General Statement: Improve programs of professional development.

        (i) (Expand and improve) programs of professional development to reflect changing manpower requirements, occupational content, and emerging career opportunities.

    c. General Statement: Identify, develop, and adopt innovative occupation-education programs.

        (i) Initiate, encourage, develop (and conduct research) of exemplary and innovative programs to enhance the quality of occupational education.

        (ii) (Increase by 50% above FY 74 funds allocated to) identify and adopt exemplary and innovative occupational education programs of other states.

(iii) (Implement an ongoing study process that involves 75% of the central and regional office staff and 20 work days, with other relevant state agency personnel and outside resources in seminars and written thematic exercises in order) to facilitate the change process in occupational education and unlock the constraints of traditionalism.

d. General Statement: Improve the placement of graduates of occupational education programs.

(i) Insure that 75% of all students enrolled in occupational education programs are placed in labor market.

(ii) Provide placement for 25% of the students in occupations related to their field of training.

(iii) (Develop 83 new instructional programs) to meet the demands for new and emerging technological occupations in order to increase post-occupational placement by 3%.

(iv) (Expand and improve the evaluation process for occupational education in order to measure program success as it relates to originally identified student aspirations) and ultimate placement in primary jobs in the labor market.

(v) Increase the number of graduates of occupational education who are placed in primary jobs by 50% of students above the FY 74 level.

(vi) Achieve a minimum level of successful placement of students in all occupational education programs so that 80% of all students either continue their education or are placed in primary jobs.

e. General Statement: Improve career-exploration programs.

(i) Develop, improve and expand educational facilities and learning environments that provide students with greater opportunities to acquire information and experiences in order to allow selection of career objectives consistent with aspirations, ability, and employment opportunities.

(ii) (Provide for a given percent of occupational-education students to participate in collaborative career-development programs.)

f. General Statement: Improve cooperative education and work-experience programs.

(i) (Further community participation) to effect educational change and program development in the occupational education field.

g. General Statement: Improve cost effectiveness of training and placement of occupation education.

(i) Reduce the cost of successfully training and placing graduates of occupational education programs to $2000 per student.

h. General Statement: Improve occupational-education programs to enhance chances of graduates continuing in general education.

(i) Increase the number of graduates of occupational education who continue in educational programs by 30% above the FY 74 level.

IV. Proximate Goals—Qualitative: Special Client Population

a. General Statement: Design special programs for handicapped.

(i) (Develop 25 special programs) designed to serve the individual needs of the handicapped in occupational education.

V. Ultimate Goals—Quantitative

a. General Statement: Increase the size and productivity of the work force through occupational education.

(i) Meet the needs of industry by providing 40% of the skilled labor force in the Commonwealth.

VI. Qualitative

No statement unless it can be inferred from the use of the words "meet needs" and "skilled" in the above statements.

Notes

Notes

Preface

1. Kenneth B. Hoyt, Rupert N. Evans, Edward F. Mackin, and Garth L. Mangum, *Career Education: What It Is and How to Do It* (Salt Lake City: Olympus Publishing Co., 2nd ed.), p. 15.

Chapter 1
Employment and Education: Immediate
Past and Future in Overview

1. International Commission on the Development of Education, *Learning to Be: The World of Education Today and Tomorrow* (Paris: UNESCO, and London: George G. Harrap & Co., Ltd., 1972).

2. Ronald E. Kutscher, "The United States Economy in 1985: Projections of GNP, Income, Output and Employment," *Monthly Labor Review* (December 1973), table 6, p. 36.

3. For example, see "Project Interact" (Boston: SRS Consultants, May 1974), Section VI, pp. 4-8, in which the potential demand for occupational training in the eastern Massachusetts region was determined to be 198,000, while the present capacity in this region for such training in vocational and trade schools and community colleges was assessed to be 12,160.

4. Bureau of Labor Statistics, *Occupational Manpower and Training Needs*, Bulletin 1824 (Washington, D.C.: U.S. Government Printing Office, 1974), table B-1, p. 80. The figure for expected annual demand is based upon data for the occupations entitled "clerical occupations."

5. Ibid., table C-1, p. 89. The figure for present annual supply is based upon data for the occupations entitled "clerical occupations."

6. Ibid., table B-1, pp. 79-87. The expected annual demand figure cited was obtained after classifying the occupations in table B-1 by the 1970 Census occupational classifications. It represents the average annual demand over the period 1972-85 for those occupations in table B-1 that would be classified as "craftsmen and kindred workers" in the 1970 Census.

7. Ibid., table C-1, pp. 88-94. The present annual supply figure cited was obtained after classifying the occupations listed in table C-1 by the 1970 Census occupational classifications. It represents the present annual supply from training programs for those occupations in table C-1 that would be classified as "craftsmen and kindred workers" in the 1970 Census.

Chapter 2
Detailed Analysis and Implications of
Projections Concerning Population, the
Economy and Education

1. Neal H. Rosenthal, "The United States Economy in 1985: Projected Changes in Occupations," *Monthly Labor Review* (December 1973), pp. 22-25.

2. National Center for Educational Statistics, *Digest of Educational Statistics 1972*, table 86, p. 74.

3. Denis F. Johnston, "The United States Economy in 1985: Population and Labor Force Projections," *Monthly Labor Review* (December 1973), p. 13.

4. Denis F. Johnston, "The Education of Workers: Projections to 1990," *Monthly Labor Review* (November 1973), p. 22.

5. President's Science Advisory Committee, *Youth: Transition to Adulthood*, p. 75.

6. Jack Alterman, "An Overview of BLS Projections," *Monthly Labor Review* (December 1973), p. 3.

7. Ibid.

8. Ronald E. Kutscher, "The United States Economy in 1985: Projections of GNP, Income, Output, and Employment," *Monthly Labor Review* (December 1973), table 5, p. 34.

9. US Bureau of the Census, *Current Population Reports*, Series P-20, No. 265, p. 19.

10. US Bureau of the Census, *Current Population Reports*, Series P-25, No. 381.

11. Alterman, "BLS Projections," p. 4.

12. Johnston, "Labor Force Projections," appendix table 1, p. 15.

13. See, for example, US Bureau of Labor Statistics, *Monthly Labor Review*, Vol. 97, No. 8 (August 1974), p. 107.

14. Ibid.

15. Anne M. Young, "The High School Class of 1972: More at Work, Fewer in College," *Monthly Labor Review*, Vol. 96, No. 6 (June 1973), table 3, p. 29.

16. National Center for Educational Statistics, *Digest of Educational Statistics 1972*, table 90, p. 76. For a good discussion of the reasons behind the recent Office of Education revision of projected college-level enrollments, see US Office of Education, *Projections of Educational Statistics to 1982-83*, pp. 15-18.

17. Johnston, "Education of Workers," table 3, p. 25.

18. Frank Newman, et al., *The Second Newman Report: National Policy and Higher Education*, (Cambridge, Mass.: The MIT Press, 1973), p. 157.

19. US Office of Education, *Projections of Educational Statistics to 1982-83*, pp. 15-16.

20. Ibid., table 5, p. 24.

21. Elizabeth Waldman and Beverly J. McEaddy, "Where Women Work: An

Analysis by Industry and Occupation," *Monthly Labor Review* (May 1974), pp. 3-7.

22. Ibid., p. 7.

23. Ibid., table 3, p. 7.

24. Ibid., table 6, p. 12.

25. Pedro Pak-tao Ng, "A Causal Approach to the Study of Satisfaction in the Academic Profession" (Doctoral dissertation, Harvard Graduate School of Education, 1971).

26. See, for example, the commentary on job and training breadth provided in James G. Scoville, *Manpower and Occupational Analysis: Concepts and Measurements* (Lexington, Mass.: D.C. Heath, Lexington Books, 1971), pp. 52-56, 60-66.

27. Robert P. Quinn, Graham L. Staines, and Margaret R. McCullough, "Job Satisfaction: Is There A Trend?" Manpower Research Monograph No. 30, U.S. Department of Labor (Washington, D.C.: U.S. Government Printing Office, 1974), pp. 37-38.

28. US Department of Labor, *1974 Manpower Report of the President*, pp. 51-52, and table F-10, p. 367.

29. Ibid., table F-2, p. 359.

30. US Bureau of the Census, *Census of Population: 1970*, Vol. 1, Characteristics of the Population, Part 23, "Massachusetts," table 20, p. 51.

31. National Center for Educational Statistics, *Digest of Educational Statistics 1972*, p. 6.

32. Massachusetts State Board of Education, *Massachusetts State Plan for Vocational Education, Fiscal Year 1974*, table 2, p. 149.

33. Ibid., table 4, p. 233.

Chapter 3
Work and Education

1. US Congress, Senate Committee on Education and Labor, *Vocational Education: Hearing on S. 619*, 79th Congress, 1st Session, May 1, 1945, p. 177.

2. Lawrence A. Cremin, *The Transformation of the School* (New York: Knopf, 1961), pp. 24-26; and John D. Runkle, "The Manual Element in Education," in *American Education and Vocationalism*, ed. Marvin Lazerson and W. Norton Grubb (New York: Teachers College Press, Columbia University, 1974), pp. 57-60.

3. David Rogers, "Vocational and Career Education: A Critique and Some New Directions," *Teachers College Record* (May 1973), pp. 490-91.

4. Stanley H. Ruttenberg and Jocelyn Gutchess, *Manpower Challenge of the 1970's: Institutions and Social Change* (Baltimore: The Johns Hopkins Press, 1971), pp. 16-23.

5. Harvard Graduate School of Education Case Files for the Administrative Career Program.

6. US Congress, Senate Committee on Education and Labor, *Vocational Education: Hearing on S. 619*, 79th Congress, 1st Session, April 30, May 1 and 2, 1945.

7. "Project Interact," (Boston: SRS Consultants, May 1974), Part 3.

8. Commission on Industrial and Technical Education, *Report of the Commission on Industrial and Technical Education*, (Boston, 1906).

9. Charles H. Winslow, comp., *Report of Committee on Industrial Education of the American Federation of Labor*, 62d Congress, 2d Session, US Senate, Document No. 936 (Washington, D.C.: 1912), p. 18.

10. Lloyd David, "Some Economic and Social Factors That Have Influenced the Development of Vocational Education in the United States" (Qualifying paper, Harvard Graduate School of Education, June 1974), p. 21.

11. "Editorial," *American Vocational Association Journal*, Vol. 10, Nos. 1 & 2, May 1935, pp. 11, 12.

12. Herbert S. Parnes, *Forecasting Educational Needs for Economic and Social Development* (Paris: OECD, the Mediterranean Regional Project, 1962); and Frederick Harbison and Charles A. Myers, *Education, Manpower and Economic Growth* (New York: McGraw-Hill, 1964).

13. Robert P. Quinn, Graham L. Staines, and Margaret R. McCullough, "Job Satisfaction: Is There A Trend?" Manpower Research Monograph No. 30. U.S. Department of Labor (Washington, D.C.: U.S. Government Printing Office, 1974), p. 1.

14. Studs Terkel, *Working* (New York: Pantheon, 1972), p. xi.

15. As reported by Richard Severo, "Survey Finds Young US Workers Increasingly Dissatisfied and Frustrated," *New York Times*, May 22, 1974, p. 45.

16. Susan Trausch, "Helping People Like Their Work," *Boston Sunday Globe*, Dec. 29, 1974, p. 49.

17. *Work in America*. A Report of a Special Task Force to the Secretary of Health, Education and Welfare, pp. 93-152.

18. H. Roy Kaplan, "How *Do* Workers View Their Work in America?" *Monthly Labor Review*, Vol. 96, No. 6 (June 1973), p. 46.

19. Quinn, Staines, and McCullough, "Job Satisfaction," pp. 3-7.

20. *Work in America*, pp. 188-201.

21. Susan Trausch, "Helping People Like Their Work," p. 49.

22. Lu Ting-yi, "Education Must Be Combined with Productive Labor," in *Chinese Communist Education: Records of the First Decade*, ed. Stewart Fraser (Nashville, Tenn.: Vanderbilt University Press, 1965), p. 294.

23. Peter J. Seybolt, "Yenan Education and the Chinese Revolution, 1937-1945" (Ph.D. dissertation, Harvard University, 1969).

24. Donald J. Munro, "Egalitarian Ideal and Educational Fact in Communist

China," in *The Political Economy of Development*, ed. Norman T. Uphoff and Warren F. Ilchman (Berkeley: University of California Press, 1972), pp. 354-64.

25. Stewart Fraser (ed.), *Chinese Communist Education: Records of the First Decade* (Nashville, Tenn.: Vanderbilt University Press, 1965).

26. Seybolt, "Yenan Education," p. 62.

27. Ibid.

28. Lu Ting-yi, "Education Must Be Combined with Productive Labor," p. 295.

29. Jeffrey Puryear, "Comparative Systems of Occupational Training in Colombia: The National Apprenticeship Service" (Ph.D. dissertation, University of Chicago, 1974), figure 1, p. 85, p. 107.

30. Records, West Bengal State Employment Office, 1973.

31. Puryear, "Occupational Training in Colombia," pp. 26-34.

Chapter 4
A Policy and Program Schema for Responding
to Education and Employment Needs

1. US Department of Labor, *1974 Manpower Report of the President*, table 1, p. 49.

2. *Work in America.* A Report of a Special Task Force to the Secretary of Health, Education, and Welfare (Cambridge: The MIT Press, 1973), pp. 188-201.

3. Studs Terkel, *Working* (New York: Pantheon, 1972).

4. Theodore Roszak, *The Making of a Counter Culture* (Garden City, New York: Anchor Books, 1969).

5. *Work in America.*

6. Rupert N. Evans, Garth L. Mangum, and Otto Pragan, *Education for Employment: The Background and Potential of the 1968 Vocational Education Amendments*, pp. 52-53.

7. Steven M. Frankel, Emily H. Allison, and Cleone L. Geddes, *Case Studies of Fifty Representative Work Education Programs.*

8. Ibid.

9. Kenneth B. Hoyt, Rupert N. Evans, Edward F. Mackin, and Garth L. Mangum, *Career Education: What It Is and How To Do It*, pp. 31-32.

10. Philadelphia Skills Center, "A Plan for the Development of Vocational Skill Centers in the City of Philadelphia," pp. 54-56.

11. Lowell S. Levin and Ann M. Martin, *Study of Manpower Needs in the Basic Health Sciences: The Development of Functional Criterion Analysis for Studies of Manpower Problems* (Washington, D.C.: Federation of American Societies for Experimental Biology, 1963).

12. Joe H. Ward, "Hierarchical Grouping to Optimize an Objective Function," *Journal of American Statistics Association* 58 (1963), pp. 236-44.

13. Laurence Wolff, Richard M. Durstine, and Christopher Davis, *Some Workforce Requirements Implied by Current Manpower Forecasts.*

14. Russell G. Davis, "Report on Calcutta Youth Self-Employment Center" (Ford Foundation: mimeo, 1972).

15. William E. Myers and Hugh W. Snyder, "Comparison of Two Career/Employment Oriented Educational Programs and the Planning Implications Inherent in Them" (Unpublished course paper, Harvard Graduate School of Education, 1974), chapter 2.

16. *Work in America,* p. 170.

17. Reports of the State Employment Service of West Bengal, 1972.

18. *New York Times* report, August 1974.

19. US Department of Labor, *1974 Manpower Report of the President,* table 1, p. 49.

20. *Work in America,* pp. 134-36.

Chapter 5
Planning, Resource Allocation, and Program
Delivery: The Legislative Base

1. "Regulations of the US Department of Labor Governing Programs Under the Comprehensive Employment and Training Act," in *Manpower Information Service, Reference File* (Washington, D.C.: The Bureau of National Affairs, Inc.), p. 91:1110.

2. Ibid. Emphasis added.

3. David Rogers, "Vocational and Career Education: A Critique and Some New Directions," *Teachers College Record* (May 1973), p. 479.

4. Lowell A. Burkett, "Latest Word from Washington," *American Vocational Journal,* Vol. 49, No. 5 (May 1974), p. 9.

Appendix B
A Summary of Major Legislation for
Work-Related Education

1. Robert Guttman, "Intergovernmental Relations Under the New Manpower Act," *Monthly Labor Review* (June 1974), p. 11.

Bibliography

Bibliography

Alterman, Jack. "An Overview of BLS Projections." *Monthly Labor Review*, December 1973, pp. 3-7.

Banta, Trudy W., Douglas C. Towne, and Linda G. Douglass. *Job Oriented Education Programs for the Disadvantaged.* No. 9 in the Series of PREP Reports. Washington, D.C.: U.S. Government Printing Office, 1972.

Banta, Trudy W., Steven M. Frankel, Sylvia M. Bowlby, and Cleone L. Geddes. *A Topical Bibliography of Work Education Programs, Projects, and Procedures.* Santa Monica, Calif.: System Development Corporation, 1973.

Barnett, Lawrence J. "Employer-Based Career Education." *The Urban Review*, March 1972, pp. 36-41.

Berg, Ivar. *Education and Jobs: The Great Training Robbery.* New York: Praeger, 1970.

Career Education Development Task Force, National Institute of Education. *Forward Plan for Career Education Research and Development.* Draft for Discussion. Washington, D.C.: April 1973.

Carnegie Commission on Higher Education. *College Graduates and Jobs: Adjusting to a New Labor Situation.* New York: McGraw-Hill, 1973.

Carnegie Commission on Higher Education. *Less Time, More Options: Education Beyond the High School.* The Carnegie Foundation for the Advancement of Teaching, 1971.

Carnegie Commission on Higher Education. *Priorities for Action: Final Report of the Carnegie Commission on Higher Education.* New York: McGraw-Hill, 1973.

David, Lloyd. "Some Economic and Social Factors That Have Influenced the Development of Vocational Education in the United States." Qualifying paper, Harvard Graduate School of Education, June 1974.

Davis, Russell G. *Forecasting for Computer Aided Career Decisions: Survey of Methodology.* Technical Memorandum No. 2. Harvard-NEEDS-Newton Information System for Vocational Decisions.

Davis, Russell G. *Planning Human Resource Development: Educational Models and Schemata.* Chicago: Rand McNally & Company, 1966.

Deuterman, William V. "Educational Attainment of Workers, March 1973." *Monthly Labor Review*, January 1974, pp. 58-62.

Eberly, Donald J. "A National Service Pilot Project." *Teachers College Record*, September 1971, pp. 65-79.

Evans, Rupert N., Garth L. Mangum, and Otto Pragan. *Education for Employment: The Background and Potential of the 1968 Vocational Education Amendments.* Ann Arbor: Institute of Labor and Industrial Relations and the National Manpower Policy Task Force, 1969.

Ferriss, Abbott L. *Indicators of Trends in American Education.* New York: Russell Sage Foundation, 1969.

Frankel, Steven M. *Executive Summary: An Assessment of School-Supervised Work Education Programs.* Santa Monica, Calif.: System Development Corporation, 1973.

_____ . *Selection Procedures Report.* Santa Monica, Calif.: System Development Corporation, 1973.

_____ , Emily Allison, and Cleone Geddes. *Case Studies of Fifty Representative Work Education Programs.* Santa Monica, Calif.: System Development Corporation, 1973.

Guttman, Robert. "Intergovernmental Relations Under the New Manpower Act." *Monthly Labor Review*, June 1974, pp. 10-16.

Harbison, Frederick, and Charles A. Myers. *Education, Manpower and Economic Growth.* New York: McGraw-Hill, 1964.

Harris, Seymour. *The Market for College Graduates.* Cambridge: Harvard University Press, 1948.

Hoyt, Kenneth B., Rupert N. Evans, Edward F. Mackin, and Garth L. Mangum. *Career Education: What It Is and How to Do It.* 2nd ed. Salt Lake City: Olympus Publishing Co., 1972.

International Commission on the Development of Education. *Learning to Be: The World of Education Today and Tomorrow.* Paris: UNESCO, and London: George G. Harrap & Co. Ltd, 1972.

Jencks, Christopher, and David Riesman. *The Academic Revolution.* New York: Doubleday, 1968.

Jencks, Christopher, et al. *Inequality.* New York: Basic Books, 1972.

Johnston, Denis F. "The Education of Workers: Projections to 1990." *Monthly Labor Review*, November 1973, pp. 22-31.

_____ . "The U.S. Labor Force: Projections to 1990." *Monthly Labor Review*, July 1973, pp. 3-13.

_____ . "The United States Economy in 1985: Population and Labor Force Projections." *Monthly Labor Review*, December 1973, pp. 8-17.

Kutscher, Ronald E. "The United States Economy in 1985: Projections of GNP, Income, Output, and Employment." *Monthly Labor Review*, December 1973, pp. 27-42.

Levin, Lowell S., and Ann M. Martin. *Study of Manpower Needs in the Basic Health Sciences: The Development of Functional Criterion Analysis for Studies of Manpower Problems.* Washington, D.C.: Federation of American Societies for Experimental Biology, 1963.

Levitan, Sar A., and Joyce K. Zickler. *The Quest for a Federal Manpower Partnership.* Cambridge: Harvard University Press, 1974.

Manpower Information, Inc. *Manpower Information Service.* Washington, D.C.: The Bureau of National Affairs.

Massachusetts State Board of Education. *Massachusetts State Plan for Vocational Education, Fiscal Year 1974.* Boston, 1973.

Mincer, Jacob. "On-the-Job Training: Costs, Returns, and Some Implications." *The Journal of Political Economy* LXX (5), Supplement, October 1962.

Munro, Donald J. "Egalitarian Ideal and Educational Fact in Communist China," in *The Political Economy of Development*, Norman T. Uphoff and Warren F. Ilchman, eds. Berkeley: University of California Press, 1972.

Myers, William E., and Hugh W. Snyder. "Comparison of Two Career/Employment-Oriented Educational Programs and the Planning Implications Inherent in Them." Course paper, Harvard Graduate School of Education, May 1974.

National and State Advisory Councils on Vocational Education. *The Impact of the Vocational Education Amendments of 1968*. Mimeographed. Prepared for Congressional Oversight Hearings, April 1974.

National Center for Educational Statistics. *Digest of Educational Statistics*. Washington, D.C.: U.S. Government Printing Office, 1973.

_____. *Students Enrolled for Advanced Degrees*. Washington, D.C.: U.S. Government Printing Office.

National Center for Health Statistics. *Vital Statistics of the United States, 1968, Volume I–Natality*. Washington, D.C.: U.S. Government Printing Office, 1970.

National Commission on the Financing of Postsecondary Education. *Financing Postsecondary Education in the United States*. Washington, D.C.: U.S. Government Printing Office, 1973.

National Science Foundation. *1969 and 1980 Science and Engineering Doctorate Supply and Utilization*. Washington, D.C.: U.S. Government Printing Office, 1971.

_____. *Unemployment Rates and Employment Characteristics for Scientists and Engineers, 1971*. Washington, D.C.: U.S. Government Printing Office, 1972.

Newman, Frank, et al. *Report on Higher Education*. Washington, D.C.: U.S. Government Printing Office, 1971.

New York (State) Commission on the Quality, Cost, and Financing of Elementary and Secondary Education in New York State. *The Fleischmann Report on the Quality, Cost, and Financing of Elementary and Secondary Education in New York State*. New York: The Viking Press, 1973.

Ng, Pedro Pak-tao. "A Causal Approach to the Study of Satisfaction in the Academic Profession." Ed.D. dissertation, Harvard Graduate School of Education, 1971.

Parnes, Herbert S. *Forecasting Educational Needs for Economic and Social Development*. Paris: OECD, the Mediterranean Project, 1962.

Perrella, Vera C. "Employment of Recent College Graduates." *Monthly Labor Review*, February 1973, pp. 41-50.

Philadelphia Skills Center. "A Plan for the Development of Vocational Skill Centers in the City of Philadelphia." Mimeographed. Philadelphia: Skills Center, n.d.

Platt, William J., Al M. Loeb, and Russell G. Davis. *Manpower and Educational Planning in Chile*. Santiago, Chile: Chile-California Program of Technical Cooperation, June 1964.

President's Science Advisory Committee. *Youth: Transition to Adulthood.* A Report of the Panel on Youth of the President's Science Advisory Committee. Washington, D.C.: U.S. Government Printing Office, 1973.

Pucinski, Roman C., and Sharlene Pearlman Hirsch, eds. *The Courage to Change: New Directions for Career Education.* Englewood Cliffs, N.J.: Prentice-Hall, Inc., 1971.

Puryear, Jeffrey. "Comparative Systems of Occupational Training in Colombia: The National Apprenticeship Service." Ph.D. dissertation, University of Chicago, 1974.

Quinn, Robert P., Graham L. Staines, and Margaret R. McCullough. "Job Satisfaction: Is There A Trend?" Manpower Research Monograph No. 30, U.S. Department of Labor. Washington, D.C.: U.S. Government Printing Office, 1974.

Rogers, David. "Vocational and Career Education: A Critique and Some New Directions." *Teachers College Record*, May 1973, pp. 471-511.

Rosenthal, Neil H. "The United States Economy in 1985: Projected Changes in Occupations." *Monthly Labor Review*, December 1973, pp. 18-26.

Ruttenberg, Stanley H., and Jocelyn Gutchess. *Manpower Challenge of the 1970's: Institutions and Social Change.* Baltimore: The Johns Hopkins Press, 1971.

Scoville, James G. *Manpower and Occupational Analysis: Concepts and Measurements.* Lexington, Mass.: D.C. Heath, Lexington Books, 1971.

Seybolt, Peter J. "Yenan Education and the Chinese Revolution, 1937-1945." Ph.D. dissertation, Harvard University, 1969.

SRS Consultants, Inc. "Project Interact." Mimeographed. Boston, May 1974.

Tarver, James D. *A Component Method of Estimating and Projecting State and Subdivisional Populations.* Stillwater, Oklahoma: Oklahoma State University, Miscellaneous Publication MP-54, 1959.

Terkel, Studs. *Working.* New York: Pantheon Books, 1972.

United Nations. *Demographic Aspects of Manpower: Report: Sex and Age Patterns of Participation in Economic Activities.* Population Studies No. 33. New York, 1962.

United Nations. *International Standard Industrial Classification of All Economic Activities.* Statistical Papers, Series M., No. 4, Rev. 1. New York: United Nations Organization.

U.S. Bureau of Labor Statistics. *College Educated Workers, 1968-80.* Bulletin 1676. Washington, D.C.: U.S. Government Printing Office.

_____. *Occupational Manpower and Training Needs.* Bulletin 1824. Washington, D.C.: U.S. Government Printing Office, 1974.

_____. *Educational Attainment of Workers.* Special Labor Force Reports Nos. 53, 65, 83, 92, 103, 125, 140, 148, 161. Washington, D.C.: U.S. Government Printing Office.

_____. *Employment of High School Graduates and Dropouts.* Special Labor

Force Report Nos. 85, 100, 108, 121, 131, 145, 155. Washington, D.C.: U.S. Government Printing Office.

_____ . *Employment of School-Age Youth*. Special Labor Force Reports Nos. 87, 98, 111, 124, 135, 147, 158. Washington, D.C.: U.S. Government Printing Office.

_____ . *Handbook of Labor Statistics 1972*. Washington, D.C.: U.S. Government Printing Office, 1972.

_____ . *Tomorrow's Manpower Needs*. Bulletin 1737. Washington, D.C.: U.S. Government Printing Office, 1971.

U.S. Bureau of the Census. *Current Population Reports*. Series P-20, Nos. 77, 99, 138, 158, 169, 182, 194, 207, 229, 243, "Educational Attainment." Washington, D.C.: U.S. Government Printing Office.

_____ . *Current Population Reports*. Series P-20, No. 247, "Population Characteristics, School Enrollment in the United States: 1972." Washington, D.C.: U.S. Government Printing Office, February 1973.

_____ . *Current Population Reports*. Series P-20, No. 252, "College Plans of High School Seniors: October 1972." Washington, D.C.: U.S. Government Printing Office, 1973.

_____ . *Current Population Reports*. Series P-20, No. 260, "Social and Economic Characteristics of Students, October 1972." Washington, D.C.: U.S. Government Printing Office, 1974.

_____ . *Current Population Reports*. Series P-20, No. 265, "Fertility Expectations of American Women: June 1973." Washington, D.C.: U.S. Government Printing Office, June 1974.

_____ . *Current Population Reports*. Series P-25, No. 381, "Projections of the Population of the United States, by Age, Sex, and Color to 1990, with Extensions of Population by Age and Sex to 2015." Washington, D.C.: U.S. Government Printing Office, December 1967.

_____ . *Current Population Reports*. Series P-25, No. 476, "Demographic Projections for the United States." Washington, D.C.: U.S. Government Printing Office, 1972.

_____ . *Current Population Reports*. Series P-25, No. 480, "Illustrative Population Projections for the United States: The Demographic Effects of Alternative Paths to Zero Growth." Washington, D.C.: U.S. Government Printing Office, April 1972.

_____ . *Current Population Reports*. Series P-25, No. 499, "Estimates of the Population of the United States and Components of Change: 1972." Washington, D.C.: U.S. Government Printing Office, 1973.

_____ . *Current Population Reports*. Series P-25, No. 519, "Estimates of the Population of the United States, by Age, Sex and Race: April 1, 1960 to July 1, 1973." Washington, D.C.: U.S. Government Printing Office, April 1974.

_____ . *Current Population Reports*. Series P-25, No. 521, "Estimates of the Population of the United States and Components of Change: 1973." Washington, D.C.: U.S. Government Printing Office, May 1974.

U.S. Bureau of the Census. *U.S. Census of Population: 1950*. Vol. IV, Special Reports, part 1, chapter B, "Occupational Characteristics." Washington, D.C.: U.S. Government Printing Office, 1956.

_____. *U.S. Census of Population: 1960*. Subject Reports, Final Report PC (2)-7A, "Occupational Characteristics." Washington, D.C.: U.S. Government Printing Office, 1963.

_____. *U.S. Census of Population: 1970*. Detailed Characteristics, Final Report PC (1)-D1, "United States Summary." Washington, D.C.: U.S. Government Printing Office, 1973.

_____. *U.S. Census of Population: 1970*. Vol. 1, Characteristics of the Population, part 23. "Massachusetts." Washington, D.C.: U.S. Government Printing Office, 1973.

_____. *U.S. Census of Population: 1970*. Subject Reports, Final Report PC (2)-5A, "School Enrollment." Washington, D.C.: U.S. Government Printing Office, 1973.

_____. *U.S. Census of Population: 1970*. Subject Reports, Final Report PC (2)-5B, "Educational Attainment." Washington, D.C.: U.S. Government Printing Office, 1973.

U.S. Department of Labor. *Breakthrough for Disadvantaged Youth*. Washington, D.C.: U.S. Government Printing Office, 1969.

_____. *1973 Manpower Report of the President*. Washington, D.C.: U.S. Government Printing Office, 1973.

_____. *1974 Manpower Report of the President*. Washington, D.C.: U.S. Government Printing Office, 1974.

U.S. Office of Education. *Opening Fall Enrollments in Higher Education*. Washington, D.C.: U.S. Government Printing Office.

_____. *Projections of Educational Statistics to 1981-82*. Washington, D.C.: U.S. Government Printing Office, 1973.

_____. *Projections of Educational Statistics to 1982-83*. Washington, D.C.: U.S. Government Printing Office, 1974.

_____. *Vocational and Technical Education, Annual Report, Fiscal Year 1969*. Washington, D.C.: U.S. Government Printing Office, 1971.

Venn, Grant. *Man, Education and Work: Postsecondary Vocational and Technical Education*. Washington, D.C.: American Council of Education, 1964.

Waldman, Elizabeth, and Beverly J. McEaddy. "Where Women Work: An Analysis by Industry and Occupation." *Monthly Labor Review*, May 1974, pp. 3-13.

Wolff, Laurence, Richard M. Durstine, and Christopher Davis. *Some Workforce Requirements Implied by Current Manpower Forecasts*. Technical Memorandum No. 4, Harvard-NEEDS-Newton Information System for Vocational Decision.

Wolfle, Dael, and Charles V. Kidd. "The Future Market for Ph.D.'s." *Science*, August 27, 1971, pp. 784-93.

Work in America. A Report of a Special Task Force to the Secretary of Health, Education and Welfare. Cambridge: The MIT Press, 1973.

Index

Index

163

About the Authors

Russell G. Davis received his graduate education at Harvard University where he is currently Professor of Education and Development. Davis teaches in the field of educational planning and has spent more than eight years working on the planning of school systems in Africa, Asia, and Latin America. He has taken leave from Harvard to serve as Director of the Asia Pacific Region of the Peace Corps, has served with USAID as regional planner for Latin America, and has served with the Ford Foundation in West Bengal. He has published fifteen books, among them novels, children's books, and technical works in the application of mathematical techniques to educational systems planning.

Gary M. Lewis has an educational background in the physical sciences, with the B.A. from Ohio Wesleyan University and the M.S. from the University of Colorado. He has been a teacher of mathematics and science at a West African teacher-training institution. Currently Lewis is a research assistant at the Center for Studies in Education and Development at the Harvard Graduate School of Education, where he received the Ed.M. degree in 1974.